Seeing FUTURE

ISBN: 979-8-9917801-1-7

Dr. Tom Sexton

Table Of Contents

Introduction……………………………......…………	1
Overview, Seeing Things To Come………………......	3
Time & God's Unfolding Plan For Man……………………	11
The Church Age………………………………….......	13
The Rapture Of The Church……………………………..	15
The Redemption Of Our Body…………………………..	17
The Judgment Seat Of Christ (Our Appointment With God)	31
Our Heavenly Reward, Gold, Silver, and Precious Stones....	39
Reward of Crowns……………………………………..	43
The Antichrist……………………………….………….	47
The Tribulation Period…………………...……………	55
The Second Coming Of Christ………………………..…	67
The Battle Of Armageddon……………………………...	71
The Millennial Rule And Reign Of Christ………………......	77
Satan's Final Rebellion……………………….…………	87
The Great White Throne Judgment……………………..	93
Hell, A Prepared Place For The Devil……………………	99
Beyond Death………………………………………….	105
Death Has Been Defeated………………………………	109
Heaven, God's Gift To Believers………………………..	113
Are We Living In The Last Days………………………..	117
Chart………………………………………………….	124
Jesus, The Only Eternity Planner………………………	125

Introduction

Jesus said, "I am Alpha and Omega, the beginning and the ending...which is, and which was, and which is to come...Write the things which thou hast seen, and the things which are, and the things which shall be hereafter;" Revelation 1:8,18-19.

Is it possible to see into the future? Is it possible to know what is coming next on planet Earth? The answer may shock you, but YES; it is possible to see into the future with the Word of God.

During the Lord Jesus' earthly ministry His disciples understood Jesus knew what was next for Israel. They asked Him a very interesting question. They asked, "saying, Tell us, when shall these things be? and what shall be the sign of thy coming, and of the end of the world?" Matthew 24:3.

While Jesus was on the earth He was looking into the future and answered their questions. Jesus helped His followers see into the future.

Join us on this wonderful journey as we look into the future of humanity. The Bible will be our guidebook to see "which is, and which was, and which is to come" and to know "the things which shall be hereafter."

★ ★ ★ ★ ★

Seeing the **FUTURE**

You will also be able to see what is beyond death for you. The Bible says, "It is appointed unto men once to die, but after this." Hebrews 9:27. What will be, "after this" in your life's future?

Paul reminded the believers in Corinth to, "let no man glory in men. For all things are yours; Whether Paul, or Apollos, or Cephas, or the world, or life, or death, or things present, or things to come; all are yours; And ye are Christ's; and Christ is God's." I Corinthians 3:21-23.

God wants His children to know what belongs to them in this world, and to know about the "things to come" for them. At the end of our study, you will be able to say with the saints of old, "I have seen the future, and can say; the best is yet to come."

"Tell us, when shall these things be?

And what *shall be* the sign of thy coming,

And of the end of the world?

Matthew 24:3

Overview, Seeing The Future

"Things To Come"

"When…the Spirit of truth, is come, he will guide you into all truth…he will shew you things to come." John 16:13

Seeing what is next, in God's plan for the ages, helps us not to lose faith and miss out on our part in God's unfolding plan for man. This is a brief overview of the major events in the future.

The Rapture Of The Church

The next great event, on God's Calander of events, is the Rapture of the church. This is when the Lord Jesus comes, as He promised, for us. At the Rapture we will receive our glorified bodies.

The Rapture of the church is the next great event in God's unfolding plan for the ages. It is important to remember that there are no signs for the Rapture of the church.

The rest of the world shall not see Him, nor realize what is happening to their friends and family members.

★ ★ ★ ★ ★

"Behold, I shew you a mystery; We shall not all sleep, but we shall all be changed, In a moment, in the twinkling of an eye, at the last trump: for the trumpet shall sound, and the dead shall be raised incorruptible, and we shall be changed. For this corruptible must put on incorruption, and this mortal must put on immortality." I Corinthians 15:51-53, (Supporting verses: I Thessalonians 4:13-18.)

The Redemption Of Our Body

Those who have died, in Christ, will receive their glorified bodies first. Then we who are alive, at the Rapture, will receive our glorified body. The redemption of our body will take place at the Rapture of the church. This is when our salvation is complete. "...for now is our salvation nearer than when we believed." Romans 13:11.

"In a moment... we shall be changed...For we know that if our earthly house of this tabernacle were dissolved, we have a building of God, an house not made with hands, eternal in the heavens." II Corinthians 5:1.

The Bible says, "Beloved, now are we the sons of God, and it doth not yet appear what we shall be: but we know that, when He shall appear, we shall be like Him; for we shall see Him as He is." I John 3:2.

The Judgment Seat Of Christ

Every Christian will appear before the Judgment Seat of Christ. We will have our glorified body, and the mind of Christ. We will think differently about the life we lived on earth.

"For we must all appear before the judgment seat of Christ; that every one may receive the things done in his body, according to that he hath done, whether it be good or bad." II Corinthians 5:10, (Supporting verses: I Corinthians 3:9-15; Romans 14:10, I John 3:1-3.)

The Marriage Supper Of The Lamb

We will be given to Christ and He will care for us and keep us for all eternity. Christ paid for our redemption on Calvary and this symbolic wedding helps us understand how dear we are to Him. We will have the marriage supper of the Lamb (Revelation 19:9).

"The kingdom of heaven is like unto a certain king, which made a marriage for his son...Then shall the kingdom of heaven be likened unto ten virgins, which took their lamps, and went forth to meet the bridegroom." Matthew 22:2, 25:1 (Supporting verses: Luke 12:35-36; John 3:27-30; II Corinthians 11:2; Ephesians 5:22-32; Jude 24.)

The Tribulation Period

The Tribulation is a seven-year period that takes place on this earth after the Rapture of the church.

This will be a time of suffering the wrath of God, which is unparalleled in human history. It is divided up into two parts, three and a half years each, the Tribulation and the Great Tribulation.

"And to wait for His Son from heaven, whom He raised from the dead, even Jesus, which delivered us from the wrath to come...then shall be great tribulation, such as was not since the beginning of the world to this time, no, nor ever shall be." Matthew 24:21, I Thessalonians 1:10, (Supporting verses: Matthew 24:29; Revelation 14:7, 10, 15:17, 16:1; Revelation 2:22, 3:10.)

The Second Coming Of Christ

The Second Coming of Christ is when He comes to this earth. It is different from the Rapture, in that, every eye shall see Him and that He comes to the earth.

No one is raptured at this coming. He comes at the end of the seven-year Tribulation period. This is referred to as His glorious appearing. (Titus 2:13).

"Immediately after the tribulation of those days shall the sun be darkened, and the moon shall not give her light, and the stars shall fall from heaven, and the powers of the heavens shall be shaken: And then shall appear the sign of the Son of man in heaven: and then shall all the tribes of the earth mourn, and they shall see the Son of man coming in the clouds of heaven with power and great glory." Matthew 24:29-30, (Supporting verses: Zechariah 14:4-8; II Thessalonians 1:7; Revelation 1:7, 11:15, 19:11-16.)

The Battle Of Armageddon

When the Lord Jesus returns to this earth, He will fight the armies of the earth who have gathered themselves together to battle against Him. This will end with the death of all unsaved people. Flesh eating birds will come and eat the dead. (Revelation 19:17-18).

"And He gathered them together into a place called in the Hebrew tongue Armageddon." Revelation 16:16, (Supporting verses: Psalm 2:1-5; Isaiah 34:1-6, 63:3-4; Joel 3:2, 9:16; Zechariah 12:2, 14:2-3, 12; Revelation 14:14-20, 19:11-21.)

Satan Bound, And The Millennial Rule And Reign Of Christ

The Millennial rule and reign of Christ will last for one thousand years. Satan will be bound for this time period and will not influence people. During this thousand-year period, Christ fulfills His promise to David and to Abraham.

"And I saw an angel come down from heaven, having the key of the bottomless pit and a great chain in his hand. And he laid hold on the dragon, that old serpent, which is the Devil, and Satan, and bound him a thousand years. And cast him into the bottomless pit. and shut him up, and set a seal upon him, that he should deceive the nations no more, till the thousand years should be fulfilled: and after that he must be loosed a little season." Revelation 20:1-3, (Supporting verses: Zechariah 14:9, 16-21; Psalm 2:6-9; Isaiah 2:2-4, 11:6-9, 65:18-23; Matthew 5:1-20, 19:27-30, 26:27-29; Mark 14:25; Luke 22:18; I Corinthians 6:9-11.)

★ ★ ★ ★ ★

Satan's Final Revolt

Satan is loosed, for a short period, at the end of the thousand-year reign of Christ. Unbelievably, Satan will manage to deceive people into following him in his final revolt against the Lord Jesus.

This final revolt ends with fire coming down from Heaven and devouring them. Satan is then cast into the lake of fire where he spends eternity. (Revelation 20:7-10).

"And when the thousand years are expired, Satan shall be loosed out of his prison. And shall go out to deceive the nations which are in the four quarters of the earth, Gog and Magog, to gather them together to battle: the number of whom is as the sand of the sea. And they went up on the breadth of the earth, and compassed the camp of the saints about, and the beloved city: and fire came down from God out of heaven, and devoured them. And the devil that deceived them was cast into the lake of fire and brimstone, where the beast and the false prophet are, and shall be tormented day and night for ever and ever." Revelation 20:7-10.

The Great White Throne Judgment

The Great White Throne Judgment is the saddest event in all human history. It will be the last time we see our unsaved friends and loved ones. All who died without Christ will be cast into the lake of fire where they will spend eternity separated from God and us.

"And I saw a great white throne, and Him that sat on it, from whose face the earth and the heaven fled away; and there was found no place for them. And I saw the dead, small and great, stand before God; and the books were opened: and another book was opened, which is the book of life....And whosoever was not found written in the book of life was cast into the lake of fire." Revelation 20:11-15, (Supporting verses: Psalm 9:17; Ecclesiastes 12:14; Daniel 7:9-10; Matthew 12:36-37; Hebrews 9:27.)

The New Heaven And New Earth

God's desire has always been to spend eternity with us. This is when it begins. He wipes away the tears from our eyes (Revelation 21:4), and He makes all things new (Revelation 21:5).

"And I saw a new heaven and a new earth: for the first heaven and the first earth were passed away; and there was no more sea." Revelation 21:1, (Supporting verses: Isaiah 65:17, 66:22; II Peter 3:13-14.)

★ ★ ★ ★ ★

Seeing the **FUTURE**

★ ★ ★ ★ ★

Time & God's Unfolding Plan For Man

"In the beginning God created the heaven and the earth. And the earth was without form, and void; and darkness *was* upon the face of the deep. And the Spirit of God moved upon the face of the waters. And God said, Let there be light: and there was light.

And God saw the light, that *it was* good: and God divided the light from the darkness. And God called the light Day, and the darkness he called Night. And the evening and the morning were the first day." Genesis 1:1-5.

We have recorded in the Word of God the beginning of Time. God started time when He created this world. We also have recorded in the Word of God the day when time is no more. God said, "there should be time no longer:" Revelation 10:6.

Down through the history of time we have the unfolding plan of God and man. God created time for man. He says man has, "A time to be born, and a time to die;" Ecclesiastes 3:2. God is eternal, He has no beginning and no end.

Seeing the FUTURE

God created man to be an eternal being. "And God said, Let us make man in our image, after our likeness: and let them have dominion over the fish of the sea, and over the fowl of the air, and over the cattle, and over all the earth, and over every creeping thing that creepeth upon the earth. So, God created man in his *own* image, in the image of God created he him; male and female created he them." Genesis 1:26-27.

God made man to be an eternal being. The Bible says, "And the LORD God formed man *of* the dust of the ground and breathed into his nostrils the breath of life; and man became a living soul." Genesis 2:7. Man was created to live forever.

Our bodies die, but we are more than just a body. People are living souls. They are body, soul, and spirit. Paul in writing the first century Christians said, "And the very God of peace sanctify you wholly; and *I pray God* your whole **spirit** and **soul** and **body** be preserved blameless unto the coming of our Lord Jesus Christ." I Thessalonians 5:23. (To read what happens when people die read the chapter, "Beyond Death")

A very brief part of a man's life is lived on earth. Our forever is lived in one of two places, in Heaven with God, or in Hell with the devil and his angels. Mans time, lived on earth, is measured in what we call, Dispensations. There are seven Dispensations of time in God's plan for man, from the Creation of Man to the Great White Throne Judgement.

In each Dispensation of time God proves man is a sinner, and will choose to sin no matter the conditions he is put in. The time in which man lives on earth, are only a brief moment in God's eternity.

The Church Age

The Dispensation of Grace

Jesus said, "Go ye into all the world, and preach the gospel to every creature." Mark 16:15.

We are living in the time of the Gentiles. The Bible says, "And when there had been much disputing, Peter rose up, and said unto them, Men *and* brethren, ye know how that a good while ago God made choice among us, that the Gentiles by my mouth should hear the word of the gospel and believe." Acts 15:7.

The Gentiles have been given their time in God's plan for man's eternity. The Bible says, "That the Gentiles should be fellow heirs, and of the same body, and partakers of his promise in Christ by the gospel:" Ephesians 3:6.

In this Dispensation, the Church age, the Lord Jesus has commissioned us, His followers, to preach the Gospel to all nations. Jesus said to His disciples, "And this gospel of the kingdom shall be preached in all the world for a witness unto all nations; and then shall the end come." Matthew 24:14. God wants all gentiles to have part in His plan for the ages. He wants us to live forever in Heaven with Him.

★★★★★

Seeing the FUTURE

The time of the Gentiles will one day be fulfilled. Jesus said Israel would suffer because of their rejecting of God's plan for their future. He said, concerning the Jewish people, "And they shall fall by the edge of the sword, and shall be led away captive into all nations: and Jerusalem shall be trodden down of the Gentiles, <u>until the times of the Gentiles be fulfilled</u>." Luke 21:24.

When the time of the Gentiles is fulfilled, the Rapture will take place, and the Church age will come to an end. Jesus also told His followers, "*Ye* hypocrites, ye can discern the face of the sky and of the earth; but how is it that ye do not discern this time?" Luke 12:56.

Our time is running out. The Bible says we need to be, "Redeeming the time, because the days are evil." Ephesians 5:16. People need to be saved. The Bible says, "For he saith, I have heard thee in a time accepted, and in the day of salvation have I succoured thee: behold, now *is* the accepted time; behold, now *is* the day of salvation." II Corinthians 6:2.

God wants to remind us, "That at that time ye were without Christ, being aliens from the commonwealth of Israel, and strangers from the covenants of promise, having no hope, and without God in the world," Ephesians 2:12. But then we became partakers of the Gospel.

How should we use our remaining time? "Walk in wisdom toward them that are without, redeeming the time." Colossians 4:5.

Share the Gospel with family and friends. Say with the Christians who have gone before us, "I am ready to preach the gospel to you that are at Rome also. For I am not ashamed of the gospel of Christ: for it is the power of God unto salvation to everyone that believeth; to the Jew first, and also to the Greek." Romans 1:15-16.

Seeing the FUTURE

THE RAPTURE OF THE CHURCH
The Shout That Changes The World

"Behold, I shew you a mystery; We shall not all sleep, but we shall all be changed," I Corinthians 15:51. (Read also, 15:51-58, I Thessalonians 4:13-18, II Thessalonians 2:1-9)

The Rapture of the church will change the world. History has recorded many events that have changed the world, but this event will put in play the coming together of the one world order. The Antichrist will step on the scene and the world will be ready for him.

The Rapture of the church is the next great event on God's calendar of events. This is when the Lord Jesus comes for His own. He said, "Let not your heart be troubled: ye believe in God, believe also in Me, In My Father's house are many mansions: if it were not so, I would have told you. I go to prepare a place for you. And if I go and prepare a place for you, I will come again and receive you unto Myself; that where I am, there ye may be also." John 14:1-3.

There is a home in Heaven being prepared for us and there is a world being prepared for the Antichrist. When the Lord comes and we go, this world will be changed. Are you ready for the Rapture?

★ ★ ★ ★ ★

The Rapture of the church takes place "In a moment, in the twinkling of an eye..." I Corinthians 15:52.

No one sees Jesus at the Rapture of the church. His coming is our "blessed hope." However, everyone sees Jesus at the Second Coming. This is His "glorious appearing." These two events are seven years apart. Today believers are, "Looking for that blessed hope,"
In the Tribulation believers will be looking for "the glorious appearing of the great God and our Saviour Jesus Christ;" Titus 2:13.

• Christ comes in the air for His own. It is the Rapture of all Christians who are taken to the Father's house. We meet Jesus "in the clouds," not on the earth.

"For the Lord himself shall descend from heaven with a shout, with the voice of the archangel, and with the trump of God: and the dead in Christ shall rise first: Then we which are alive and remain shall be caught up together with them in the clouds, to meet the Lord in the air: and so shall we ever be with the Lord." I Thessalonians. 4:16-17.

• There are no signs for the Rapture of the church, it could happen at any moment.

"Be ye therefore ready also: for the Son of man cometh at an hour when ye think not." Luke 12:40.

• The Rapture is for believers only and it is a time of great joy.

THE RAPTURE OF THE CHURCH

"Then <u>we</u> which are alive and remain shall be caught up together with them in the clouds, to meet the Lord in the air: and so shall we ever be with the Lord." 1Thessalonians. 4:17.

- The Judgment Seat of Christ takes place in Heaven after the Rapture of the Church.

"For we must all appear before the judgment seat of Christ; that every one may receive the things done in his body, according to that he hath done, whether it be good or bad." II Corinthians 5:10.

- Only <u>believers</u> will see Jesus at the Rapture.

"In a moment, in the twinkling of an eye, at the last trump: for the trumpet shall sound, and the dead shall be raised incorruptible, and we shall be changed." 1Corinthians 15:52.

- The Rapture takes place <u>before</u> the "day of wrath." (The Tribulation period).

"Because thou hast kept the word of my patience, I also will keep thee from the hour of temptation, which shall come upon all the world, to try them that dwell upon the earth." Revelation 3:10.

- The Tribulation begins <u>after</u> the Rapture.

The Bible says that the Holy Spirit will "be taken out of the way. And then shall that Wicked be revealed..." II Thessalonians 2: 7-8.

★ ★ ★ ★ ★

We are witnessing the world being prepared for all that Jesus said would happen <u>after</u> the Rapture of the church takes place. In other words, the stage is now being set for the "rulers of darkness" to carry out their plan of death and destruction.

The Bible says, "We wrestle not against flesh and blood, but against principalities, against powers, against the <u>rulers of the darkness</u> of this world, against spiritual wickedness in high places." Ephesians 6:12. We also read that, "Evil men and seducers shall wax worse and worse, deceiving, and being deceived." II Timothy 3:13.

The Rapture of the church is "that blessed hope" every believer has in his heart. Looking for the coming of the Lord helps us to live right, at home and in public.

My beloved pastor, Dr. Lee Roberson, would often say, "Looking for the Lord's return is one of the secrets of keeping good relationships in one's life."

Who Will Be Raptured?

The Lord Jesus will come for those who have put their faith and trust in Him. "But thanks be to God, which giveth us the victory through our Lord Jesus Christ." I Corinthians 15:57. Jesus said, "I go and prepare a place for you..." John 14:1-3. We will meet believers who have died and gone on to Heaven, in the air.

Believers, who are alive when Christ comes, will be caught up together with them. "For the Lord Himself shall descend from heaven with a shout, with the voice of the archangel, and with the trump of God: and the dead in Christ shall rise first: Then we which are alive and remain shall be caught up together with them in the clouds, to meet the Lord in the air: and so shall we ever be with the Lord." I Thessalonians 4:16-17.

Those who are raised from the dead will say, "...O grave, where is thy victory?" Those who are alive and are caught up to meet the Lord in the air will say, "O death, where is thy sting?..." (I Corinthians 15:55). Both the dead in Christ and all living Christians will be taken out of this world at the Rapture.

When Will The Rapture Take Place?

Jesus said He will come when, "the times of the Gentiles be fulfilled." Luke 21:24. In other words, there is a time on Gods calendar when our time is up, and the time of the gentiles is fulfilled.
No wonder Jesus said, "I must work the works of him that sent me, while it is day: the night cometh, when no man can work." John 9:4. Our day to work in the Lord's work and to reach our generation, is coming to an end.

★ ★ ★ ★ ★

Only the Father knows when the Rapture will take place. Jesus said, "But of that day and hour knoweth no man, no, not the angels of heaven, but My Father only." Matthew 24:36. The Father will tell the Son, "Go get your bride."

Jesus will come when the bride of Christ is complete. (The last soul is saved) "And I John saw the holy city, new Jerusalem, coming down from God out of heaven, prepared as a bride adorned for her husband." Revelation 21:2. The church is the bride of Christ and He is preparing a place in Heaven for all who have put their faith and trust in Him. When the last soul is saved and the bride is complete, then the Father in Heaven will say it is time.

Jesus will come when Heaven is prepared. Jesus said, "In My Father's house are many mansions: if it were not so, I would have told you. I go to prepare a place for you." John 14:2. As Heaven is being prepared for believers, the world is being prepared for the Antichrist and his lie.

Which kingdom are we giving our life and treasures to build?

Why The Rapture Is So World Changing?

What is the aftermath of the Rapture? What will the world be like after the Rapture? How many people will be gone?

All believers will be taken at the Rapture. "Then we which are alive and remain shall be caught up together with them in the clouds, to meet the Lord in the air: and so shall we ever be with the Lord." I Thessalonians 4:17. Those who have heard the Gospel and put their faith in Christ will be taken up.

The Rapture will happen without a trace. "In a moment, in the twinkling of an eye, at the last trump: for the trumpet shall sound, and the dead shall be raised incorruptible, and we shall be changed." I Corinthians 15:52. Millions will be missing without a trace. This is why it is important to understand the difference between the Rapture of the church and the Second Coming of Christ.

At His Second Coming every eye, shall see Him. The Second Coming of Christ is "the glorious appearing of the great God and our Saviour Jesus Christ." Titus 2:13.

The world will be in shock because of the millions of missing people. Remember the Rapture takes place so quickly that no one sees it happen. "In a moment, in the twinkling of an eye."

The Holy Spirit will be taken out of the way. "For the mystery of iniquity doth already work: only he who now letteth will let, until he be taken out of the way." II Thessalonians 2:7. This verse teaches us that now the Holy Spirit is holding back much evil, but after the Rapture He will be, "taken out of the way," and evil will be unleashed on earth.

The world will be different when Christians and the Holy Spirit are taken out of the way. It will become like the days of Noah and Lot.

The Antichrist, that Wicked one, will be revealed. "For the mystery of iniquity doth already work: only he who now letteth will let, until he be taken out of the way. And then shall that Wicked be revealed, whom the Lord shall consume with the spirit of His mouth, and shall destroy with the brightness of His coming:" II Thessalonians 2:8. Believers have always asked, "Who is the Antichrist?"

No one will know who the Antichrist is until the Rapture of the church. However, because Satan does not know when the Rapture will take place, he must have someone prepared in every generation. (More will be covered on this in a future chapter)

Preparing For The Rapture?

"Therefore, my beloved brethren, be ye stedfast, unmoveable, always abounding in the work of the Lord, forasmuch as ye know that your labour is not in vain in the Lord." I Corinthians 15:58.

Be ready to meet the Lord. "Beloved, now are we the sons of God, and it doth not yet appear what we shall be: but we know that, when He shall appear, we shall be like Him; for we shall see Him as He is. And every man that hath this hope in him purifieth himself, even as He is pure." I John 3:2-3. The Rapture of the church is one of the great motives for the believer to live right and to reach others.

Carry on in the work God has given us to do.
Jesus said we should, "Work...while it is day: the night cometh, when no man can work." John 9:4. We must work while the Lord is working. He is working today.

Paul said, "I ceased not to warn every one night and day with tears." Acts 20:31.

Here are three questions that helps us prepare for our Heavenly meeting with Jesus:
- Are you in Christ? (II Corinthians 5:17)
- How far are you in? (Philippians 1:21)
- Are you trying to get others in? (Romans 9:1-3)

> "All that will live godly in
> Christ Jesus
> shall suffer persecution.
> But evil men and seducers shall
> wax worse and worse,
> deceiving, and being deceived.
> But continue thou in the things
> which thou hast learned
> and hast been assured of,
> knowing of whom
> thou hast learned *them*."
>
> II Timothy 3:12-14

★ ★ ★ ★ ★

Seeing the FUTURE

Carry On

In Christ we are more than conquers.
In Him, every battle is won.
So, carry on in the faith once delivered,
Holding up the crucified one.

Rulers of darkness are making advancements,
Lying ahead are the souls of lost men.
Very soon the battle will be raging,
With His power and the Gospel we'll win.

The only hope for the world is the Gospel,
By His power the Good News we tell.
Unto us He has given a great promise,
Upon this rock, hell's gates shall not prevail.

The weapons of warfare to us are given,
The stronghold of evil cannot stand.
The mighty army of the Lord is empowered,
From the enemy we'll take back our land.

There'll be a wedding in that golden city,
In Heaven where the saints now abide.
So, get ready we're going up in the Rapture,
When the Father says, "Son, go get your bride."

The Lord's return is the hope of all believers,
When we'll join our loved ones who have gone.
Oh, sorrow not as others who are hopeless,
The Lord will shout, and we'll be going home.

Carry on in the faith once delivered,
Carry on in the spirit of one accord.
Carry on to a world that is waiting,
Carry on with the shield and the sword.

The Redemption Of Our Body

The Bible says, "For we know that if our earthly house of this tabernacle were dissolved, we have a building of God, an house not made with hands, eternal in the heavens." II Corinthians 5:1. John in his writings said, "Beloved, now are we the sons of God, and it doth not yet appear what we shall be: but we know that, when He shall appear, we shall be like Him; for we shall see Him as He is." I John 3:2.

The redemption of our body, according to the Bible, is going to happen, "In a moment…we shall be changed." I Corinthians 15:52.

Those who have died, in Christ, will receive their glorified bodies first. Then we who are alive at the Rapture will receive our glorified body. The redemption of our body will take place at the Rapture of the church.

This is when our salvation is complete. "For now is our salvation nearer than when we believed." Romans 13:11.

★ ★ ★ ★ ★

Our Salvation Is Complete When We Receive Our Glorified Body. The Bible says Jesus, "delivered us from so great a death, and doth deliver: in whom we trust that he will yet deliver us...Who shall change our vile body, that it may be fashioned like unto his glorious body, according to the working whereby he is able even to subdue all things unto himself." II Corinthians 1:10, Philippians 3:21.

The word "fashioned" means that we will fit in Heaven. Our body will be conformed to heavens standards.

We are saved from the <u>penalty</u> of sin. Romans 8:1. We are being saved from the <u>practice</u> of sin. I Corinthians 9:27. We will one day be saved from the very <u>presence</u> of sin, when we receive our glorified body, "So when this corruptible shall have put on incorruption, and this mortal shall have put on immortality, then shall be brought to pass the saying that is written, Death is swallowed up in victory." I Corinthians 15:54.

Our Glorified Body Will Be Like Jesus'. "Beloved, now are we the sons of God, and it doth not yet appear what we shall be: but we know that, when He shall appear, we shall be like Him; for we shall see Him as He is." I John 3:2. What more could a believer want than to be like Jesus?

THE REDEMPTION OF OUR BODY

It will be a recognizable body. "And, behold, there appeared unto them Moses and Elias talking with Him." Matthew 17:3. We will know and recognize each other in Heaven. The disciples were able to see that people still look like themselves in Heaven.

It is a glorious body. "For… the glory which shall be revealed in us. I Corinthians 15:47. "The first man is of the earth, earthy: the second man is the Lord from heaven." Romans 8:18. This means that we will be able to be in God's presence and live. We will enjoy fellowship with God like Adam and Eve did before the fall.

It is an eternal body. "For we know that if our earthly house of this tabernacle were dissolved, we have a building of God, an house not made with hands, eternal in the heavens." II Corinthians 5:1. We will never die nor will we ever experience sickness or disease.

It will be a body without limitations. "And after eight days again His disciples were within, and Thomas with them: then came Jesus, the doors being shut, and stood in the midst, and said, Peace be unto you." John 20:26. Our glorified body will not be limited by time, space or gravity. It is a body where the spirit, not the flesh, is dominant.

★ ★ ★ ★ ★

Seeing the FUTURE

It is a body with the mind of Christ. "Let this mind be in you, which was also in Christ Jesus…then shall I know even as also I am known." Philippians 2:5, I Corinthians 13:12. We will not think like we think now. We will look back on our lives and the opportunities God gave us, with the mind of Christ.

> "Beloved, now are we the sons of God,
> and it doth not yet appear what we shall be:
> but we know that, when He shall appear,
> we shall be like Him;
> for we shall see Him as He is."
> I John 3:2

The Judgment Set Of CHRIST
Our Appointment With God

"For we must all appear before the judgment seat of Christ; that every one may receive the things done in his body, according to that he hath done, whether it be good or bad." II Corinthians 5:10.

The Judgment Seat of Christ is the most important day in the believer's life. It is our appointment with God. It is a day when every child of God will give an account of their life. This great day should have a powerful effect on our lives today. This great event should help all Christians stay on track with the plan and purpose God has for them.

The Body We Appear In

"We shall be like Him; for we shall see Him as He is." I John 3:2.

Our glorified body will have the mind of Christ. We will not think like we think today. We will see our life with a whole new perspective.

The Book That Records Our Lives

"Thou tellest my wanderings...in Thy book?" Psalm 56:8. The Lord has kept track of all of our deeds, as a Christian. There is nothing that has gone unnoticed. One day we will see our life as a story told. I hope you like the story of your life. Remember our life's record has the "good" and the "bad."

The Basis For Our Judgment

"Every man's work shall be made manifest: for the day shall declare it, because it shall be revealed by fire; and the fire shall try every man's work of what sort it is." I Corinthians 3:13. The little word "sort" means what kind of work. It refers to the motives behind our work, whether it is good or bad.

The areas we will give an account of are too many to list. Here are just a few.

How faithful were we? "Moreover it is required in stewards, that a man be found faithful." I Corinthians 4:2. Did we stick with it, or did we throw in the towel when things got tough? Will we hear the Lord Jesus say, "well done?"

How did we use our money? "But this I say, He which soweth sparingly shall reap also sparingly; and he which soweth bountifully shall reap also bountifully." II Corinthians 9:6-7. (I Corinthians 16:2, I Timothy 6:17-19)

★ ★ ★ ★ ★

THE JUDGEMENT SEAT OF CHRIST

Did we love money or did we love Jesus and use money? How much did we invest in the Gospel?

How did we use our God given talent and abilities? "…For unto whomsoever much is given, of him shall be much required…" Luke 12:48. We all have something that is needed in the Lord's work. You are a treasure, a gift to the church. (Romans 12:1-2, I Corinthians 12:4)

How faithful were we to the Word of God? "I charge thee therefore before God, and the Lord Jesus Christ,.. Preach the word; be instant in season, out of season; reprove, rebuke, exhort with all longsuffering and doctrine." II Timothy 4:1-2. (Acts 20:26-28, II Timothy 4:1-2, I Peter 5:2-4) What we do with the Word of God will determine what the Lord does with us.

How faithful were we to sharing our faith? "The fruit of the righteous is a tree of life; and he that winneth souls is wise." Proverbs 11:30. "And they that be wise shall shine as the brightness of the firmament; and they that turn many to righteousness as the stars for ever and ever." Daniel 12:3.

It is more important to be a faithful witness than it is to be a soul winner. A faithful witness will talk to everyone and will also win souls.

How well did we love and treat other Christians? "For God is not unrighteous to forget your work and labour of love, which ye have shewed toward His name, in that ye have ministered to the saints…" Hebrews 6:10. (Matthew 25: 35-36, Luke 12:13-14)

★ ★ ★ ★ ★

Do we love and encourage Christians, or do we discourage God's people?

How closely did we follow the plan God had chosen for our life? "Let us run with patience the race that is set before us, Looking unto Jesus the author and finisher of our faith." Hebrews 12:1-2. Remember the Lord wants us to finish the race. It is more important to end right than to be the first to finish.

How much did we suffer for Christ? "There is no man that hath left house, or brethren, or sisters, or father, or mother, or wife, or children, or lands, for my sake, and the gospel's, But he shall receive an hundredfold now ..and in the world to come eternal life." Mark 10:29-30. (Matthew 5:11-12, Romans 8:18, I Peter 4:12-13, II Corinthians 4:17)

There will be a measure of suffering as we serve the Lord. The closer we get to the coming of the Lord, the more trouble we will encounter.

How much did we love the coming of Christ? "Henceforth there is laid up for me a crown of righteousness, which the Lord, the righteous judge, shall give me at that day: and not to me only, but unto all them also that love his appearing." II Timothy 4:8.

Think of a young child, that is waiting and looking for their father to come home, knowing he is bringing a gift for them. They would love his appearing.

★ ★ ★ ★ ★

THE JUDGEMENT SEAT OF CHRIST

How did we respond to temptation and sin? "But I keep under my body, and bring it into subjection: lest that by any means, when I have preached to others, I myself should be a castaway." I Corinthians 9:27. (James 1:2-3, Revelation 2:10, I Corinthians 9:25-27)

Everyone is tempted. It is how we respond to temptation that reveals our character.

How did we use our influence? "For none of us liveth to himself, and no man dieth to himself." Romans 14:7-8. Influence may be the area that we receive our greatest reward, because influence lives beyond the grave.

How much did we pray? "And when He had taken the book, the four beasts and four and twenty elders fell down before the Lamb, having every one of them harps, and golden vials full of odours, which are the prayers of saints." Revelation 5:8. (I Thessalonians 5:17, I Timothy 2:1) One day we will see how much we have prayed.

Every prayer that we have prayed will be poured out for all to see.

It would be impossible to make a list of all the areas in which we will give an account, on that day. The very thoughts and desires of our heart will be revealed. We will not only give an account of what we did with our life, but we will give an account of what we could have done for Christ.

★ ★ ★ ★ ★

Seeing the FUTURE

I wrote a poem about people who build their lives on the sands of this world, and never think about their appointment with Jesus.

> "Moreover as for me,
> God forbid that I should sin
> against the LORD in
> ceasing to pray for you:
> but I will teach you the good
> and the right way."
>
> I Samuel 12:23

Living In The Land of Nod

There's a place in the Bible called "the land of Nod,"

It's where Cain chose to live

Away from the presence of God.

People are moving there from around the world,

But Nod is no place to raise a little boy or girl.

It's true, in Nod, you live life the way you please,

And everyone in Nod enjoys their days with such ease.

There's no one in Nod telling you how you should be,

But there's a darkness about Nod not everyone sees.

You see, Nod is not really a land without a <u>god</u>,

It's our Heavenly Father who's not welcome in Nod.

Nod is a life consumed with gaining silver and gold,

It's a place we exist capturing heart, mind, and soul.

Living a season in Nod "seemeth right unto a man,"

Enjoying "the pleasures of sin"

And not following God's plan.

One day all the treasures of Nod will go up in flames,

Kingdom's men have built will all burn the same.

So, before you build your life in this strange land,

Remember, everything built in Nod is built on sand.

Seeing the **FUTURE**

Our Heavenly Reward

Jesus said, "And, behold, I come quickly; and My reward is with Me, to give every man according as his work shall be." Revelation 22:12. "It is written, Eye hath not seen, nor ear heard, neither have entered into the heart of man, the things which God hath prepared for them that love Him." I Corinthians 2:9.

As we study this subject, let us remember that it is impossible for us to know all that God has for us. The basis of our reward is determined by how much we gave our lives to Christ and the Gospel.

"Gold, Silver and Precious Stones"

The Bible says, about our life's work, that "if any man build upon this foundation gold, silver, precious stones, wood, hay, stubble; Every man's work shall be made manifest: for the day shall declare it, because it shall be revealed by fire; and the fire shall try every man's work of what sort it is. If any man's work abide which he hath built thereupon, he shall receive a reward." I Corinthians 3:12-14.

Our Heavenly reward is based on our work being tested by fire. "If any man's work abide which he hath built thereupon, he shall receive a reward." If it goes through the fire, we "receive a reward."

★ ★ ★ ★ ★

No one knows all that the Lord has in store for His children. However, we do know how our life's work will be judged. It will be judged by, "what sort it is." It will not be judged by what size it is.

Wood Hay and Stubble

If it is the right "sort" of work, we will receive a reward. If our work is not of the right "sort," it will burn as, "wood, hay, stubble" would burn. That means it was done for the wrong reason or done the wrong way.

Gold, Silver, and Precious Stones

Gold represents love. Our highest motive for service is love. Christians who work together, because they love Jesus, accomplish much more for God with their life. What we have done with our life for Christ, out of a motive of love, will be Gold at the Judgement Seat of Christ. "For the love of Christ constraineth us; because we thus judge, that if one died for all, then were all dead:" II Corinthians 5:17.

Silver at the Judgement Seat of Christ represents investment in the redemption of the lost: the investment of our time, talent, and treasure in giving out the Gospel to the lost. Hosea said about Gomah, "So I bought her to me for fifteen pieces of silver," Hosea 3:2. Hosea showed his love for his wife Gomah, when he redeemed her for fifteen pieces of silver. Silver at the Judgement Seat of Christ represents our going and investing in the redemption of the lost. Our personal investment of time, talent, and treasure in giving out the Gospel to the lost, is silver.

Precious Stones represents the time and love we have given to help Christians have a good day when they see Jesus. Who can we say about, "I thank my God upon every remembrance of you," and "I have you in my heart"? In other words, who have we poured our life into? That will be, "precious stones" one day.

★ ★ ★ ★ ★

Seeing the **FUTURE**

★ ★ ★ ★ ★

The Reward Of Crowns

The Bible teaches us that there are crowns to be given to believers for their faithfulness and their suffering. Will you receive a crown at His appearing?

The Crown of Life

"Blessed is the man that endureth temptation: for when he is tried, he shall receive the crown of life, which the Lord hath promised to them that love Him." James 1:12-15. (Revelation 2:10, 3:11) The Crown of Life is given to those who live victoriously over temptation. Temptation is part of the Christian life. The Bible says, "every man is tempted." James 1:14. It is when we yield to temptation that we fail. Do not take that first step.

The Crown of Righteousness

"Henceforth there is laid up for me a crown of righteousness, which the Lord, the righteous judge, shall give me at that day: and not to me only, but unto all them also that love His appearing." II Timothy 4:8. The Crown of Righteousness is given to those who love His appearing. What would make someone love His appearing? (Read Matt.6:19-20)

★ ★ ★ ★ ★

The Crown of Glory

"Feed the flock of God which is among you,...And when the chief Shepherd shall appear, ye shall receive a crown of glory that fadeth not away." I Peter 5:2&4. The Crown of Glory is given to those who faithfully teach God's Word. This crown is not just for preachers and teachers, it is for all believers. (Read Matthew 19-20)

The Crown of Incorruption

"And every man that striveth for the mastery is temperate in all things. Now they do it to obtain a corruptible crown; but we an incorruptible." I Corinthians 9:25. (Hebrews 12:1-2, Philippians 3:13-14) The Crown of Incorruption is given to those who run the race with singleness of purpose. This is for those who do not get off track with their life.

The Crown of Rejoicing

"For what is our hope, or joy, or crown of rejoicing? Are not even ye in the presence of our Lord Jesus Christ at His coming? For ye are our glory and joy." I Thessalonians 2:19-20. The Crown of Rejoicing is given to those who are a faithful witness and soul winner. These two additional verses help us understand the importance of being a faithful witness.

"The fruit of the righteous is a tree of life; and he that winneth souls is wise." Proverbs 11:30. "And they that be wise shall shine as the brightness of the firmament; and they that turn many to righteousness as the stars for ever and ever." Daniel 12:3. The Lord Jesus is always ready to go with us.

What are we going to do with the crowns we receive? The Bible says in "The four and twenty elders fall down before him that sat on the throne, and worship him that liveth for ever and ever, and cast their crowns before the throne, saying, Thou art worthy, O Lord, to receive glory and honour and power: for thou hast created all things, and for thy pleasure they are and were created." Revelation 4:10-11.

According to the Bible we are going to cast our crowns at the feet of Jesus. No one wants to meet the Lord Jesus emptied handed. The hymn, "Must I Go, And Empty Handed" is a powerful truth for all believers.

★ ★ ★ ★ ★

Seeing the FUTURE

"I thank my God
upon every remembrance of you…
in every prayer of mine…with joy,
For your fellowship in the gospel…
Being confident of this very thing,
that he which hath begun
a good work in you will
perform *it* until the day of
Jesus Christ…
Because I have you in my heart.

Do all things
without murmurings and disputings:
That ye may be blameless and harmless,
the sons of God, without rebuke,
in the midst of a crooked
and perverse nation,
among whom ye shine as
lights in the world;
Holding forth the word of life;
that I may rejoice
in the day of Christ,
that I have not run in vain,
neither laboured in vain."
Philippians 1:1-6, 2:14-16

The Antichrist
"That Wicked One"

The world is looking for a leader. Will they find someone who they believe will lead them out of the crisis they are facing? Will they find the leader that they are looking for? God's Word teaches us that they will find such a man. "Even him, whose coming is after the working of Satan with all power and signs and lying wonders," This man is the Antichrist, the "Wicked" one. II Thessalonians 2:8-9.

John wrote, "Little children, it is the last time: and as ye have heard that antichrist shall come, even now are there many antichrists; whereby we know that it is the last time." I John 2:18.

We live in a day when there is the "…spirit of antichrist…in the world." I John 4:3. For there are "…many deceivers…who confess not that Jesus Christ is come in the flesh. This is a deceiver and an antichrist." II John 1:7. But there is coming that one who is empowered by Satan, the one who is <u>the</u> Antichrist. Is he alive today? Who is he? How will we recognize him? For the answer to these questions and many others, we turn to the Word of God. This we know, "…the time is at hand." Revelation 1:3, 22:10.

★ ★ ★ ★ ★

The Antichrist will not step on the scene until after the Rapture of the church. There will be such great heartbreak and fear that he will appear to be the answer everyone is looking for. It is impossible for anyone to know who he is until God's timing allows him to be revealed; but there are some basic questions that can be answered.

Where Does He Come From?

"And I will put enmity between thee and the woman, and between thy seed and her seed, it shall bruise thy head, and thou shalt bruise his heel." Genesis 3:15.

There will be a mystery surrounding his birth. We know that there are questions we will not find the answers to until we see Jesus. We know that Satan has something to do with his birth. He will be hidden until it is time for him to be revealed. "And then shall that Wicked be revealed." II Thessalonians 2:8.

The life that he lives before he is revealed will be admirable. The Antichrist will also have those who will prepare the way for him. Because of the way that he comes on the scene, most people will believe that he is Christ. "And many false prophets shall rise, and shall deceive many." Matthew 24:11.

Why Does He Come?

"Even him, whose coming is after the working of Satan with all power and signs and lying wonders," II Thessalonians 2:9. He comes to do...the working of Satan..." The Antichrist comes to do the work of the evil one. He comes to destroy lives. "He was a murderer from the beginning." John 8:44.

Christ came to do the will of the Father. Jesus said, "My meat is to do the will of him that sent me, and to finish his work." John 4:34. The Lord Jesus came to give life; the Antichrist comes to destroy lives. Jesus said, "The thief cometh not, but for to steal, and to kill, and to destroy. I am come that they might have life, and that they might have it more abundantly." John 10:10.

How Will The Antichrist Be Able To Accomplish His Goal?

"For there shall arise false Christs, and false prophets, and shall shew great signs and wonders; insomuch that, if it were possible, they shall deceive the very elect." Matthew 24:24.

Satan gives him power. The Antichrist will be able to deceive people and take control of the world. He will be empowered by Satan. "...the dragon gave him his power..." Revelation 13:2. The Bible says, "Even him, whose coming is after the working of Satan with all power and signs and lying wonders." II Thessalonians 2:9.

★ ★ ★ ★ ★

Seeing the FUTURE

We have examples of the devil empowering men in the Old Testament. Paul in his writing told us who the evil men were who challenged Moses in Pharaoh's court. He said, "Now as Jannes and Jambres withstood Moses, so do these also resist the truth: men of corrupt minds, reprobate concerning the faith." II Timothy 3:8.

These men "...Jannes and Jambres..." were given power by the devil to deceive people (Exodus 4:1-5, 7:8-13).

World leaders will give him power. "These have one mind, and shall give their power and strength unto the beast." Revelation 17:12-13. He will be empowered by Satan and the world leaders will give him total control. This world is looking for someone that they believe will be able to solve the problems they are facing and to lead them to a one world order.

The world will find a man that they will give "...their power and strength unto..." Revelation 17:11.

The Antichrist will be a great communicator. "And the king shall do according to his will; and he shall exalt himself, and magnify himself above every god, and shall speak marvellous things against the God of gods, and shall prosper till the indignation be accomplished: for that that is determined shall be done." He will be able to "...speak marvellous things..." Daniel 11:36.

The Lord Jesus said that if it were possible he would "...deceive the very elect." Matthew 24:24. The Antichrist will speak with "...lying wonders..." II Thessalonians 2:9. The reason he will not be able to deceive Christians is because believers are with Jesus in Heaven.

Political and religious leaders will follow the Antichrist. The Bible says, "and power was given him over all kindreds, and tongues, and nations And all that dwell upon the earth shall worship him..." It is interesting that he "...speaks marvellous things against the God of gods..." Revelation 13:7-8, Daniel 11:36.

All the religious leaders and all the political leaders will be deceived by him. He will have control over the world's military "And it was given unto him to make war with the saints..." Revelation 13:7. (also Daniel 9:27, Revelation 19:19). Remember the goal of the Antichrist and the evil one is to destroy God's people. All through human history Satan has been at "...war with the saints...", but here is a time when he is in control of all the armies of the earth.

The Antichrist takes control over the food and finances of the world. The Bible says, "And that no man might buy or sell, save he that had the mark, or the name of the beast, or the number of his name." Revelation 13:17. He does this with the "Mark of the Beast." Our generation has more understanding of how easily this could be done, better than any other generation who has lived before us.

★ ★ ★ ★ ★

What Should We Be Doing?

1. Don't lose faith, these things must come to pass. Jesus said these things, shall be the sign of His coming. (Matthew 24:3) Remember the scriptures cannot be broken (John 10:35); they must be fulfilled. (John 17:12; 19:24)

2. Look beyond the troubles of life. Jesus said, "These things I have spoken unto you, that in me ye might have peace. In the world ye shall have tribulation: but be of good cheer; I have overcome the world." John 16:33. "...I will come again..." John 14:3. We (the church) will be with the LORD before all these things come into play. "I...will keep thee from the hour of temptation, which shall come upon all the world, to try them that dwell upon the earth." Revelation 3:10.

3. Live for Christ today. Paul said, "For to me to live is Christ, and to die is gain...and all that will live godly in Christ Jesus shall suffer persecution." Philippians 1:21; II Timothy 3:12. Trouble and heartache is part of the Christian life. But, "we are more than conquerors through him that loved us." Romans 8:37. We are on the winning side.

4. Keep Looking, Jesus is Coming.
The angels told the people who saw Jesus go up in the clouds, "Ye men of Galilee, why stand ye gazing up into heaven? this same Jesus, which is taken up from you into heaven, shall so come in like manner as ye have seen him go into heaven." Acts 1:11.

★★★★★

The Lord Jesus said, "I will come again." John 14:3. We are closer to the coming of the LORD today, than we have ever been in human history. "So… when ye see these things come to pass, know ye that the kingdom of God is nigh at hand." Luke 21:31.

Jesus said,

"In the world ye shall have tribulation:

But be of good cheer;

I have overcome the world."

John 16:33

"And the world passeth away,
and the lust thereof:
but he that doeth the will of God
abideth for ever."

I John 2:17

★ ★ ★ ★ ★

Seeing the FUTURE

★ ★ ★ ★ ★

The Tribulation Period

"For then shall be great tribulation, such as was not since the beginning of the world to this time, no, nor ever shall be. And except those days should be shortened, there should no flesh be saved: but for the elect's sake those days shall be shortened." Matthew 24:21-24.

The Tribulation begins after the Rapture of the church and covers a period of seven years. The first half is called the Tribulation and the second half is called the Great Tribulation.

There are some main events, that take place in each, that helps us to understand why one is called the Tribulation and the other the Great Tribulation.

People will be terrified. There will be unanswered questions about what has happened concerning the Rapture of the church.

The Lord Jesus promised He would come for us before the hour of temptation. He said, "I also will keep thee from the hour of temptation, which shall come upon all the world, to try them that dwell upon the earth." Revelation 3:10.

★ ★ ★ ★ ★

Today many are being deceived by the devil and are departing from the faith, giving heed to seducing spirits, and doctrines of devils. But during the Tribulation the Antichrist will be able to deceive the world. How can people be so deceived? Christians will be in Heaven with Jesus and the Holy Spirit will be taken out of the way.

The Bible says, "For the mystery of iniquity doth already work: only He (the Holy Spirit) who now letteth will let, until He be taken out of the way. And then shall that Wicked be revealed," II Thessalonians 2:7-8.

Today the work of the Holy Spirit is to "...reprove the world of sin, and of righteousness, and of judgment:" John 16:7-8. To "reprove" means to convict. He convicts the world of sin. He helps people realize they are guilty before God. In the Tribulation period He will not hold back wickedness.

The Antichrist Is Revealed

"And then shall that Wicked be revealed, whom the Lord shall consume with the spirit of His mouth, and shall destroy with the brightness of His coming:" II Thessalonians 2:8.

There have been many false prophets that have claimed they are Christ (Matthew 24:5), but this one is the Antichrist. He will be empowered by Satan and will deceive the hearts of people. The Antichrist will seek to destroy the Jewish people and God's judgment will be poured out on the earth. This is called, "the time of Jacob's trouble." Jeremiah 30:7.

All of God's creation will be affected by the judgment which is poured out by God during this time. We are living in a day of great light and are able to understand these things. But after the church is raptured and the Holy Spirit is removed, the world will be in spiritual darkness. After the Rapture of the church the Day of the Lord's wrath will begin.

The Day Of The Lord's Wrath Will Begin

The Bible says, "The great day of the LORD is near, it is…a day of wrath, a day of trouble and distress, a day of wasteness and desolation, a day of darkness and gloominess, a day of clouds and thick darkness, A day of the trumpet and alarm against the fenced cities, and against the high towers.

And I will bring distress upon men, that they shall walk like blind men, because they have sinned against the LORD: and their blood shall be poured out as dust, and their flesh as the dung. Neither their silver nor their gold shall be able to deliver them in the day of the LORD'S wrath…" Zephaniah 1:14-18.

The Tribulation period, which is called, "the Day of the LORD'S wrath" according to Zephaniah 1:18. It is a seven-year period that centers around the nation of Israel and relates especially to the Jews which have gone back to their land in unbelief. A covenant will be made with the Jews for temple worship, and in the middle of the seven years the covenant will be broken.

The Bible says, "they shall run to and fro to seek the word of the LORD, and shall not find it." Amos 8:12. Although these events and judgments are clearly given in the Bible, we must remember that during the Tribulation period there will be a famine of the very Word of God.

How will creation be affected during the Great Tribulation?

"Therefore I will shake the heavens, and the earth shall remove out of her place, in the wrath of the LORD of hosts, and in the day of his fierce anger." Isaiah 13:13.

There will be great earthquakes. "And I beheld when he had opened the sixth seal, and, lo, there was a great earthquake…" Revelation 6:12.

There will be tidal waves and ocean disasters. "And the second angel poured out his vial upon the sea; and it became as the blood of a dead man: and every living soul died in the sea." Revelation 16:3.

The water on the earth will become polluted. "And the third angel poured out his vial upon the rivers and fountains of waters; and they became blood." Revelation 16:3-4.

There will be scorching heat and uncontrolled fires. "And the fourth angel poured out his vial upon the sun; and power was given unto him to scorch men with fire. And men were scorched with great heat, and blasphemed the name of God, which hath power over these plagues: and they repented not to give him glory." Revelation 16:8-9.

People believe in global warming and fail to see that this is **global <u>warning</u>** telling them to prepare to meet God.

The earth will rock to and fro. "Behold, the LORD maketh the earth empty, and maketh it waste, and turneth it upside down, and scattereth abroad the inhabitants thereof." Isaiah 24:1, "The earth shall reel to and fro like a drunkard, and shall be removed like a cottage;…" Isaiah 24:19-20.

There will be fearful heavenly signs and disturbances. "And there shall be signs in the sun, and in the moon, and in the stars;" Luke 21:25. (Revelation 6:12-14, 8, 12-13.)

The stars, moon and sun will be darkened. "For the stars of heaven and the constellations thereof shall not give their light: the sun shall be darkened in his going forth, and the moon shall not cause her light to shine." Isaiah 13:10. (Joel 2:30-31, 3:15; Revelation 8:12-13.)

★ ★ ★ ★ ★

Seeing the FUTURE

There will be a thick darkness over the earth. "...and his kingdom was full of darkness;" Joel 2:2, Revelation 16:10.

The moon will be turned into blood. "...the moon became as blood;" Revelation 6:12.

Massive hailstones of fire will fall upon the earth. "...there followed hail and fire mingled with blood, and they were cast upon the earth: and the third part of trees was burnt up, and all green grass was burnt up...there fell a great star from heaven." Revelation 8:7,10.

"And the stars of heaven fell unto the earth...And there fell upon men a great hail out of heaven, every stone about the weight of a talent." Revelation 6:13,16:21.

The heavens rolled together like a scroll. "the heavens shall be rolled together as a scroll:" Isaiah 34:4.

People will face unparalleled trouble. "I will consume man and beast;" Zephaniah 1:3.

There will be bloody wars. "And ye shall hear of wars and rumours of wars:" Matthew 24:6.
There will be drunkenness on the earth. "For as in the days that were before the flood they were eating and drinking." Matthew 24:38.

Men will hide in caves and rocks in fear of God. "And the kings of the earth, and the great men, and the rich men, and the chief captains, and the mighty men, and every bondman, and every free man, hid themselves in the dens and in the rocks of the mountains;" Revelation 6:15.

There will be worldwide famines. "...to kill... with hunger..." Revelation 6:8.

There will be a great slaughter of people by beasts. "...to kill...with the beasts of the earth." Revelation 6:8.

There will be a demonic invasion. "And he opened the bottomless pit; And there came out of the smoke locusts upon the earth ...and their teeth were as the teeth of lions...there were stings in their tails:" Revelation 9:2-3,8,10.

People will be plagued with cancerous sores. "...and there fell a noisome and grievous sore upon the men which had the mark of the beast, and upon them which worshipped his image." Revelation 16:2.

"And this shall be the plague wherewith the LORD will smite all the people that have fought against Jerusalem; Their flesh shall consume away while they stand upon their feet, and their eyes shall consume away in their holes, and their tongue shall consume away in their mouth." Zechariah 14:12.

★ ★ ★ ★ ★

With no Christians, who are the light of the world, (Matthew 5:16) and no Holy Spirit to convict of wrong and right; people will welcome someone who seems to have answers for the troubles of their lives.

The world is crying," Leave us alone!" God and His people are saying, "I will not give you up." During the Tribulation period the world will have freedom to do everything they have ever desired to do.

During this time, called the Tribulation, we see men continue to reject God and His love for their sinful pleasures. Why do so many people choose to "enjoy the pleasures of sin for a season"? Do they not know the season of sin is very short?

Moses chose God and His people. The Bible says concerning his choice, that he would "rather to suffer affliction with the people of God, than to enjoy the pleasures of sin for a season." Hebrews 11:25 Who have you chosen?

Israel In The Tribulation

Jesus said about the Tribulation period, "Nation shall rise against nation, and kingdom against kingdom: and there shall be famines, and pestilences, and earthquakes, in divers places. All these *are* the beginning of sorrows. Then shall they deliver you up to be afflicted, and shall kill you: and ye shall be hated of all nations for my name's sake." Matthew 24:7-9.

THE TRIBULATION PERIOD

The Lord Jesus said there would be a time, in Israel's future, that they would be "hated of all nations." We have witnessed a hatred of Israel growing in our day. But during the Tribulation the hatred of Israel grows worldwide. For the first half (3½ years) of the Tribulation, the goal of complete destruction of Israel, is concealed by the Antichrist.

After the Rapture of the Church there will be worldwide violence, and "Nation shall rise against nation," as Jesus said. However, the Antichrist has a plan of peace that all nations will accept. The Bible says, "It is not good to accept the person of the wicked, to overthrow the righteous in judgment." Proverbs 18:5. By the time Israel realizes this peace plan was Satan's plan for their complete destruction, it is too late.

Now the Antichrist turns on Israel, and all the nations on earth join in on the total destruction of Israel. They have been deceived into believing that killing all the Jews will solve the world's problems.

Why does Satan hate Israel, and why must the Jews die?

★ ★ ★ ★ ★

Seeing the FUTURE

First, the Jewish people gave us Jesus. The Bible tells us that, "When the fulness of the time was come, God sent forth his Son, made of a woman, made under the law, To redeem them that were under the law, that we might receive the adoption of sons." Galatians 4:4-5. The woman God used to give the world Jesus was Mary, a Jew.

The Devil has been at war with women ever since God told him that the "seed" of the woman would destroy his power and kingdom. Genisis 3:15. The devil hates women and he hates the Jews.

Second, God made a promise to Abraham that one day his decedents would cover the earth. God said to Abraham, "I will make thy seed to multiply as the <u>stars of heaven</u>, and will give unto thy seed all these countries; and in thy seed shall all the nations of the earth be blessed;" Genisis 26:4.
This promise has not yet been fulfilled, but it will be during the "Millennial Rule and Reign of Christ" on earth.

The descendants of Abraham will populate the earth as the "stars of heaven". If the Antichrist and his armies kill all the Jewish people, during the Tribulation, God cannot keep His promise to Abraham. "Now to Abraham and his seed were the promises made." Galatians 3:16.

★ ★ ★ ★ ★

Third, God also made a promise to David that has yet to be fulfilled. God said, "I have made a covenant with my chosen, I have sworn unto David my servant, Thy seed will I establish for ever, and build up thy throne to all generations." Psalm 89:3-4.

"And, behold, thou shalt conceive in thy womb, and bring forth a son, and shalt call his name JESUS. He shall be great, and shall be called the Son of the Highest: and the Lord God shall give unto him the throne of his father David: And he shall reign over the house of Jacob for ever; and of his kingdom there shall be no end." Luke 1:31-33.

Jesus is the one who will set on the throne of Daivd. It is in Christ that all the promises God made to David will be fulfilled. The Tribulation period will end just before the Jewish people, the descendants of Abraham and David, are destroyed. The devil has, all down through the centuries, tried to stop God's plan for man.

If Satan can stop God from fulfilling one promise, He made to Israel, he has won. It is in the seven-year Tribulation period that Satan's last effort is defeated.

"Woe to the inhabiters of the earth and of the sea! for the devil is come down unto you, having great wrath, because he knoweth that he hath but a short time." Revelation 12:12.

★ ★ ★ ★ ★

Seeing the **FUTURE**

> Jesus said, "
> And great earthquakes
> shall be in divers places,
> and famines, and pestilences;
> and fearful sights and great signs
> shall there be from heaven."
>
> Luke 21:11

> "Immediately after the tribulation
> of those days shall the sun be darkened,
> and the moon shall not give her light,
> and the stars shall fall from heaven,
> and the powers of the heavens
> shall be shaken:"
>
> Matthew 24:29

The Second Coming Of CHRIST

"Behold, He cometh with clouds; and every eye shall see Him, and they also which pierced him: and all kindreds of the earth shall wail because of him. Even so, Amen." Revelation 1:7. (Matthew 24:15:31, Revelation 19:11-20:6)

The Second Coming of Christ, "the glorious appearing of the great God and our Saviour Jesus Christ," Titus 2:13, takes place seven years after the Rapture of the church. Knowing the difference between the Rapture of the church and the Second Coming of Christ helps us to understand the times in which we live. There are no signs for the Rapture of the church, but there are many signs for the Second Coming of Christ.

We sometimes, in our thoughts and teaching, get the Rapture of the church confused with the Second Coming of Christ. There are no prophecies or events left to be fulfilled before Christ calls the church away. The Rapture could take place at any moment. At the Rapture of the church, Christ meets us in the air.

"Then we which are alive and remain shall be caught up together with them in the clouds, to meet the Lord in the air:" I Thessalonians 4:17.

★ ★ ★ ★ ★

Seeing the **FUTURE**

The Second Coming of Christ will take place seven years after the Rapture of the church and there are several prophecies that must be fulfilled before Christ comes again to this earth.

Many of the signs we see in this world today point to the Second Coming of Christ, not the Rapture of the church.

Therefore, because we live in a time in human history where the signs of the times point to Christ's return, we believe we are truly living in the last great days of the church age.

Again, let me say, no one sees Jesus at the Rapture of the church. His coming is our "blessed hope." However, everyone sees Jesus at the Second Coming. This is His "glorious appearing." These two events are seven years apart. Today believers are, "Looking for that blessed hope." In the Tribulation believers will be looking for "the glorious appearing of the great God and our Saviour Jesus Christ;" Titus 2:13.

- Every eye will see Him at the Second Coming.

"Behold, he cometh with clouds; and every eye shall see him, and they also which pierced him: and all kindreds of the earth shall wail because of him. Even so, Amen." Revelation 1:7.

- The Second Coming is when Christ comes with His own to the earth and no one is raptured.

"And then shall appear the sign of the Son of man in heaven: and then shall all the tribes of the earth mourn, and they shall see the Son of man coming in the clouds of heaven with power and great glory." Matthew 24:30.

• The Second Coming of Christ occurs seven years after the Rapture and there are many signs for Christ's physical coming.

"And when these things begin to come to pass, then look up, and lift up your heads; for your redemption draweth nigh." Luke 21:28.

• The Second Coming of Christ affects all humanity and is a time of great mourning.

"And said to the mountains and rocks, Fall on us, and hide us from the face of him that sitteth on the throne, and from the wrath of the Lamb: For the great day of his wrath is come; and who shall be able to stand?" Revelation 6:16-17.

• The Second Coming takes place at the end of the Tribulation.

"And when these things begin to come to pass, then look up, and lift up your heads; for your redemption draweth nigh." Luke 21:28.

• Satan will be bound in the abyss for 1,000 years when Christ comes.

★ ★ ★ ★ ★

Seeing the FUTURE

"And he laid hold on the dragon, that old serpent, which is the Devil, and Satan, and bound him a thousand years." Revelation 20:2.

> "Looking for that blessed hope, and the glorious appearing of the great God and our Saviour Jesus Christ."
> Titus 2:13

The Battle Of Armageddon

"And he gathered them together into a place called in the Hebrew tongue Armageddon." Revelation 16:16.

"And I saw the beast, and the kings of the earth, and their armies, gathered together to make war against him that sat on the horse, and against his army...And the remnant were slain with the sword of him that sat upon the horse, which sword proceeded out of his mouth: and all the fowls were filled with their flesh." Revelation 19:19-21. (Supporting verses, Daniel 11:40-45, Joel 3:9-17, Zechariah 14:1-3)

The battle of Armageddon will be the last great world war in human history. This battle will take place in the closing days of the Tribulation period. The Antichrist will gather his forces together to destroy the Jewish people. The Antichrist attempts the total annihilation of all Jews. His plan would work except for the fact that the Lord Jesus has chosen this time in human history to return to this earth.

"And then shall appear the sign of the Son of man in heaven: and then shall all the tribes of the earth mourn, and they shall see the Son of man coming in the clouds of heaven with power and great glory." Matthew 24:30.

Seeing the FUTURE

The nation of Israel rejected Christ during His earthly ministry, but will accept Him when He comes just before they are destroyed by the Antichrist and his armies. This is the Second Coming of Christ, when every eye shall see Him.

Questions to consider in helping us understand this great event in human history:

What Is This Battle All About?

"Assemble yourselves, and come, all ye heathen, and gather yourselves together round about: thither cause thy mighty ones to come down, O LORD...The LORD also shall roar out of Zion, and utter His voice from Jerusalem; and the heavens and the earth shall shake: but the LORD will be the hope of His people, and the strength of the children of Israel." Joel 3:11,17.

"When ye therefore shall see the abomination of desolation, spoken of by Daniel the prophet, stand in the holy place, (whoso readeth, let him understand:)" Matthew 24:15.

Satan wants to see "the abomination" of every good thing that God has done. This is the ultimate battle between good and evil. It is after the temple is defiled, that the Jewish people flee from Jerusalem.

The Antichrist will gather his armies together to destroy God's people. (Psalm 2:1-6, Revelation 16:12-16)

★ ★ ★ ★ ★

The Lord Jesus said that Israel would one day be hated of all nations. This is a fulfillment of that prophecy. Satan has a goal to destroy the Jews and end God's covenant with Abraham and David.

The Antichrist would succeed except, "the LORD will be the hope of His people" Joel 3:16.

The Lord Jesus said, "For I say unto you, Ye shall not see Me henceforth, till ye shall say, Blessed is He that cometh in the name of the Lord." Matthew 23:39. The Lord Jesus returns to save the descendants of Abraham.

Where Will This Battle Take Place?

Matthew 24:16, "Then let them which be in Judaea flee into the mountains:" "I will also gather all nations, and will bring them down into the valley of Jehoshaphat, and will plead with them there for My people and for My heritage Israel, whom they have scattered among the nations, and parted My land." Joel 3:2.

"Let the heathen be wakened, and come up to the valley of Jehoshaphat: for there will I sit to judge all the heathen round about." Joel 3:12.

This battle will take place in Israel. The site where this will occur is the plain around the hill of Megiddo, in northern Israel, about twenty miles southwest of Haifa. Although this battle takes place in one location, there will be people killed around the world.

★ ★ ★ ★ ★

The people who receive the mark of the beast will have sealed their doom. (Revelation 14:9-10)

It is hard for us to imagine why someone would receive this mark or join an army that wants to kill God's people and fight against the Lord Jesus. Today we are told that there are people from over 100 nations who have joined the fight against Israel and Christians in the middle east. Who would have believed?

When Will It Take Place?

"And I saw heaven opened, and behold a white horse; and He that sat upon him was called Faithful and True, and in righteousness

He doth judge and make war...And out of His mouth goeth a sharp sword, that with it He should smite the nations: and He shall rule them with a rod of iron: and He treadeth the winepress of the fierceness and wrath of Almighty God. And He hath on His vesture and on His thigh a name written, KING OF KINGS, AND LORD OF LORDS." Revelation 19:11,15-16.

This battle will take place at the close of the Tribulation period. This will be seven years after the Rapture of the church. We must remember that believers all around the earth will be killed during the Tribulation period.

THE BATTLE OF ARMAGEDDON

"And it was given unto him to make war with the saints, and to overcome them: and power was given him over all kindreds, and tongues, and nations." Revelation 13:7. The final great battle to end the war against the saints.

How Will It End?

"And the remnant were slain with the sword of Him that sat upon the horse, which sword proceeded out of His mouth: and all the fowls were filled with their flesh." Revelation 19:21.

It will end with the death of all who fight against the Lord.

"And I saw an angel standing in the sun; and he cried with a loud voice, saying to all the fowls that fly in the midst of heaven, Come and gather yourselves together unto the supper of the great God; That ye may eat the flesh of kings, and the flesh of captains, and the flesh of mighty men, and the flesh of horses, and of them that sit on them, and the flesh of all men, both free and bond, both small and great." Revelation 19:17-18.

The Bible says, "the fowls were filled with their flesh." This truly is a great sad supper. Think about your friends and loved ones being part of this sad supper. Never in all of human history has there ever been such a loss of life.

★ ★ ★ ★ ★

Why Is This So Important?

"And I saw an angel come down from heaven, having the key of the bottomless pit and a great chain in his hand. And he laid hold on the dragon, that old serpent, which is the Devil, and Satan, and bound him a thousand years, And cast him into the bottomless pit, and shut him up, and set a seal upon him, that he should deceive the nations no more, till the thousand years should be fulfilled: and after that he must be loosed a little season." Revelation 20:1-3.

The battle of Armageddon ends the Tribulation period and a new dispensation begins. This is when Christ sets up His kingdom on the earth and rules and reigns for one thousand years. Those who fled Jerusalem, when the temple was defiled, were not killed by the Antichrist and his armies. (Matthew 24:13-18)

Believers, who lived through the Tribulation period, are the ones who enter the Millennium with Christ and repopulate the earth. They have not received their glorified body, which means they will have children born in this new age.

The Millennial Rule And Reign Of CHRIST

"And I saw thrones, and they sat upon them, and judgment was given unto them: and I saw the souls of them that were beheaded for the witness of Jesus, and for the word of God, and which had not worshipped the beast, neither his image, neither had received his mark upon their foreheads, or in their hands; and they lived and reigned with Christ a thousand years." Revelation 20:4.

The literal rule and reign of Christ on this earth is part of God's plan for the ages. These 1000 years of perfect rule will conclude with a rebellion toward God and will prove that no matter what the conditions, man is a sinner and will choose to rebel when given the chance. This dispensation of the Millennial reign of Christ is the last and final dispensation. Man's responsibility is to obey Christ. This dispensation ends with man's failure. Proving that no matter what the condition, man is a hopeless sinner.

★ ★ ★ ★ ★

Satan Is Removed During The Reign of Christ

"And I saw an angel come down from heaven, having the key of the bottomless pit and a great chain in his hand. And he laid hold on the dragon, that old serpent, which is the Devil, and Satan, and bound him a thousand years, And cast him into the bottomless pit, and shut him up, and set a seal upon him, that he should deceive the nations no more, till the thousand years should be fulfilled: and after that he must be loosed a little season." Revelation 20:1-3.

After the battle of Armageddon, the Lord will set up His kingdom on this earth. There will be one thousand years of peace.

This will be the last dispensation of time. This is possible because Satan is removed. He will be bound for one thousand years. Once the thousand years are complete, he will then be loosed for a brief season.

"And when the thousand years are expired, Satan shall be loosed out of his prison." Revelation 20:7. He will find those who choose to rebel against the Lord Jesus.

THE MILLENNIAL RULE AND REIGN OF CHRIST

God's Promises to Abraham
(Abrahamic Covenant)

God said to Abraham, "And I will make thy seed as the dust of the earth: so that if a man can number the dust of the earth, then shall thy seed also be numbered." Genesis 13:16. "The remnant shall return, even the remnant of Jacob, unto the mighty God." Isaiah 10:21. "And ye shall be My people, and I will be your God." Jeremiah 30:22.

During the Millennium the earth will be repopulated with the seed of Abraham. Because the curse on Adam will be lifted, there will be no death during the Millennial Reign of Christ. The Jewish people, who are the seed of Abraham, are alive when the Lord Jesus returns.

They will enter the Millennium in their natural bodies and repopulate the earth.

God always keeps His promises. The Lord Jesus said, "Heaven and earth shall pass away, but My words shall not pass away. "Matthew 24:35.

God's promise made to David
(Davidic Covenant)

"And, behold, thou shalt conceive in thy womb, and bring forth a son, and shalt call His name JESUS. He shall be great, and shall be called the Son of the Highest: and the Lord God shall give unto Him the throne of His father David: And He shall reign over the house of Jacob for ever; and of His kingdom there shall be no end." Luke 1:31-33. (Other scriptures: Acts 15:15-16; Isaiah 11:1-2; 55:3-11; Jeremiah 23:5-8.)

★ ★ ★ ★ ★

God promised that the Son of David would sit on the throne and rule the earth. This will happen in the Millennium. "The book of the generation of Jesus Christ, the son of David..." Matthew 1:1. This verse, along with many others, helps us to see that the Lord Jesus is "...the son of David..."

Every generation of believers have been very interested in this covenant, God made with David, because it has much to do with our position in the literal rule and reign of Christ upon this earth. "If we suffer, we shall also reign with him: if we deny him, he also will deny us:" II Timothy 2:12.

The Bible says, "Blessed and holy *is* he that hath part in the first resurrection: on such the second death hath no power, but they shall be priests of God and of Christ, and shall reign with him a thousand years." Revelation 20:6.

We must remember that these two covenants, that God made with Abraham and with David, are unconditional.

The Lord Jesus Sits On The Throne

Believers have a part in the kingdom reign "with Christ a thousand years." Revelation 20:4.

This one thousand years is about Christ, and God's promise to David. Mary was reminded of this promise when she became the mother of Jesus. The angel said, "He shall be great, and shall be called the Son of the Highest: and the Lord God shall give unto him the throne of his father David: And he shall reign over the house of Jacob forever; and of his kingdom there shall be no end. Luke 1:32-33.

The Bible says, "Jesus Christ our Lord...was made of the seed of David according to the flesh." Romans 1:3. The Lord Christ, "the seed of David," is the one who makes this kingdom great. He will rule from Jerusalem. God said, "Yet have I set My king upon My holy hill of Zion." Psalm 2:6.

The World during the Reign of Christ.

"And many people shall go and say, Come ye, and let us go up to the mountain of the LORD, to the house of the God of Jacob; and He will teach us of His ways, and we will walk in His paths: for out of Zion shall go forth the law, and the word of the LORD from Jerusalem." Isaiah 2:3.

"But with righteousness shall He judge the poor, and reprove with equity for the meek of the earth: and He shall smite the earth with the rod of His mouth, and with the breath of His lips shall He slay the wicked." Isaiah 11:4.

★ ★ ★ ★ ★

Seeing the **FUTURE**

There will be peace on the earth during the reign of Christ. There are those who believe that if we do things better, people will do better. The thousand years ends with a rebellion against the Lord Jesus.

The curse upon creation will be removed

"And unto Adam....cursed is the ground for thy sake; in sorrow shalt thou eat of it all the days of thy life... In the sweat of thy face shalt thou eat bread, till thou return unto the ground; for out of it wast thou taken: for dust thou art, and unto dust shalt thou return." Genesis 3:17-19.

The whole earth will be affected by the presence of Christ. The curse is removed.

The animal kingdom will be at peace

"The wolf also shall dwell with the lamb, and the leopard shall lie down with the kid; and the calf and the young lion and the fatling together; and a little child shall lead them. And the cow and the bear shall feed; their young ones shall lie down together: and the lion shall eat straw like the ox." Isaiah 11:6-7.

The very nature of the animal kingdom will be changed. They will not kill and eat each other.

THE MILLENNIAL RULE AND REIGN OF CHRIST

All sickness will be removed

There will be no need of doctors or hospitals. The Bible says, "And the inhabitant shall not say, I am sick:…" Isaiah 33:24. "For I will restore health unto thee, and I will heal thee of thy wounds,…" Jeremiah 30:17. "…and will strengthen that which was sick:…" Ezekiel 34:16.

Physical death will be swallowed up

"He will swallow up death in victory;…" Isaiah 25:8. With no death and no sickness, the world's population will increase faster than ever in human history. Abraham's seed will cover the earth.

"And in that day shall the deaf hear the words of the book, and the eyes of the blind shall see out of obscurity, and out of darkness." Isaiah 29:18. (Also Isaiah 29:18, 35:5-6, 61:1-2; Jeremiah 31:8)

Babies will be born perfect.

The longevity of man will be restored

"There shall be no more thence an infant of days, nor an old man that hath not filled his days: for the child shall die an hundred years old; but the sinner being an hundred years old shall be accursed." Isaiah 65:20. Think about how many birthdays people will celebrate.

Man's knowledge of God will increase

"For the earth shall be filled with the knowledge of the glory of the LORD, as the waters cover the sea." Habakkuk 2:14.

★ ★ ★ ★ ★

"And it shall come to pass in that day, saith the LORD of hosts, that I will cut off the names of the idols out of the land, and they shall no more be remembered: and also I will cause the prophets and the unclean spirit to pass out of the land." Zechariah 13:2.

Evil is removed from the earth.

There will be worldwide peace

"And He shall judge among the nations, and… nation shall not lift up sword against nation, neither shall they learn war any more." Isaiah 2:4.

"And My people shall dwell in a peaceable habitation, and in sure dwellings, and in quiet resting places;" Isaiah 32:18. A world at peace, because of the Prince of Peace. There will be no fear.

Who Are The People On Earth With Christ?

"Blessed and holy is he that hath part in the first resurrection: on such the second death hath no power, but they shall be priests of God and of Christ, and shall reign with Him a thousand years." Revelation 20:6. There are three groups of people in the Millennium.

1. The Tribulation saints, who were alive at the coming of Christ.

They do not have their glorified body. They are the ones who will repopulate the earth. Their children will accept or reject the Gospel. "And the streets of the city shall be full of boys and girls playing in the streets thereof." Zechariah 8:5.

2. The Tribulation saints who were killed during the Tribulation.

They have their glorified bodies and will not have children.

3. The church age saints.

They received their glorified body at the Rapture. "And hast made us unto our God kings and priests: and we shall reign on the earth." Revelation 5:10.

The Tribulation saints who were killed during the Tribulation period and the church age saints will not be repopulating the earth.

We, who have been faithful in serving God, will rule and reign with Christ during His Millennial kingdom. (To understand what we will be doing, we must understand the parable of the talent. Luke 19:11-27)

"And Jesus said unto them, Verily I say unto you, That ye which have followed Me, in the regeneration when the Son of man shall sit in the throne of His glory, ye also shall sit upon twelve thrones, judging the twelve tribes of Israel." Matthew 19:28.

Paul said, "Do ye not know that the saints shall judge the world?" I Corinthians 6:2. "If we suffer, we shall also reign with Him: if we deny Him, He also will deny us:" II Timothy 2:12.

★ ★ ★ ★ ★

"The wolf also shall dwell with the lamb, and the leopard shall lie down with the kid; and the calf and the young lion and the fatling together; and a little child shall lead them.

The wolf and the lamb shall feed together, and the lion shall eat straw like the bullock: and dust *shall be* the serpent's meat. They shall not hurt nor destroy in all my holy mountain, saith the LORD."

Isaiah 11:6, 65:25

Satan's Final Rebellion

"And when the thousand years are expired, Satan shall be loosed out of his prison, And shall go out to deceive the nations which are in the four quarters of the earth...And the devil that deceived them was cast into the lake of fire and brimstone, where the beast and the false prophet are, and shall be tormented day and night for ever and ever." Revelation 20:7-10.

Satan's final rebellion is recorded in our text. This is the end of his thousands of years of causing heartache and destruction. All through the centuries he has destroyed the lives of people. He has been bound for one thousand years in the bottomless pit.

During the thousand years, with Christ on the throne in His kingdom, Satan has not been able to deceive people. Now he has been loosed for a season to tempt and deceive those who were born during the Millennial rule and reign of Christ. He gathers people from all four corners of the world to join his rebellion. They are destroyed by God with fire from heaven. "And... fire came down from God out of heaven, and devoured them." Revelation 20:9. Satan is then cast into the lake of fire where he will spend eternity.

★ ★ ★ ★ ★

Satan's Beginning

"Thou was perfect in thy ways from the day that thou wast created, till iniquity was found in thee." Ezekiel 28:14-15.

He was created for a good work. "Thou wast perfect in thy ways from the day that thou wast created,..." Ezekiel 28:15a.

He was once an angel of light. "And no marvel; for Satan himself is transformed into an angel of light." II Corinthians 11:14.

He was beautiful before his fall. "Thine heart was lifted up because of thy beauty." Ezekiel 28:17.

He was given music. "...the workmanship of thy tabrets and of thy pipes was prepared in thee in the day that thou wast created." Ezekiel 28:13. Satan was created by God and was a beautiful angel of light and music.

He chose to rebel against God.

"How art thou fallen from heaven, O Lucifer; son of the morning! how art thou cut down to the ground... For thou hast said in thine heart, I will ascend into heaven, I will exalt my throne above the stars of God...I will be like the most High. Yet thou shalt be brought down to hell, to the sides of the pit." Isaiah 14:12-15.

He became the power of darkness. "To open their eyes, and to turn them from darkness to light, and from the power of Satan unto God, that they may receive forgiveness of sins, and inheritance among them which are sanctified by faith that is in Me." Acts 26:18. Jesus said, "this is your hour; and the power of darkness." Luke 22:53.

He lost his beauty. "...till iniquity was found in thee." Ezekiel 28:15b.

His music has become perverted. "Now if ye be ready that at what time ye hear the sound of ... all kinds of musick, ye fall down and worship the image which I have made;" Daniel 3:15. This music was inspired by Satan. When Satan fell, his role changed. The kingdom of light is headed up by our Lord and Saviour Jesus Christ. John 1:9 The kingdom of darkness is headed up by "the devil and his angels:" Matthew 25:41.

One third of the angels in heaven fell when Satan fell. "And his tail drew the third part of the stars of heaven, and did cast them to the earth:..." Revelation 12:4.

Satan's Defeat

"And I will put enmity between thee and the woman, and between thy seed and her seed; it shall bruise thy head, and thou shalt bruise his heel." Genesis 3:15.

★ ★ ★ ★ ★

The Lord Jesus Defeated Satan On Calvary.

"Forasmuch then as the children are partakers of flesh and blood, He also Himself likewise took part of the same; that through death He might destroy him that had the power of death, that is, the devil;" Hebrews 2:14.

The power of Satan's kingdom was broken when Christ rose from the grave. "I am He that liveth, and was dead; and, behold, I am alive for evermore. Amen; and have the keys of hell and of death." Revelation 1:18.

The Lord Jesus broke the devil's kingdom and bound the strong man (who is Satan). "How can one enter into a strong man's house, and spoil his goods, except he first bind the strong man? and then he will spoil his house." Matthew 12:29.

Satan gathers an army to fight Christ at the end of the thousand years. "And shall go out to deceive the nations which are in the four quarters of the earth, Gog and Magog,to gather them together to battle: the number of whom is as the sand of the sea." Revelation 20:8.

What does Satan say that deceives people and causes them to rebel against God? He tells them the same old lies:
- He tells people that God does not love them.
- He causes people to doubt God's Word.

- He tells people that rebellion does not cost you anything.

Satan's army is destroyed by God. "And they went up on the breadth of the earth, and compassed the camp of the saints about, and the beloved city: and fire came down from God out of heaven, and devoured them." Revelation 20:9.

Satan Is Cast Into The Lake Of Fire.

"And the devil that deceived them was cast into the lake of fire and brimstone, where the beast and the false prophet are, and shall be tormented day and night for ever and ever." Revelation 20:10. Satan's rebellion, which began in Heaven, ends with him being cast into the lake of fire, never to be seen or heard of again.

Seeing the **FUTURE**

★ ★ ★ ★ ★

The Great White Throne Judgment
The Saddest Day In Human History

"And I saw a great white throne, and Him that sat on it, from whose face the earth and the heaven fled away; and there was found no place for them. And I saw the dead, small and great, stand before God; and the books were opened: and another book was opened, which is the book of life: and the dead were judged out of those things which were written in the books, according to their works.

And the sea gave up the dead which were in it; and death and hell delivered up the dead which were in them: and they were judged every man according to their works. And death and hell were cast into the lake of fire. This is the second death. And whosoever was not found written in the book of life was cast into the lake of fire." Revelation 20:11-15.

The Great White Throne Judgment is the saddest day in all human history. Remember, this is <u>before</u> God wipes away our tears. The Bible says**,** "And God shall wipe away all tears from their eyes; and there shall be no more death, neither sorrow, nor crying, neither shall there be any more pain: for the former things are passed away. (Revelation 21:4).

★ ★ ★ ★ ★

Seeing the FUTURE

We will see in that day, the result of people rejecting the Gospel, who said no to God's love and forgiveness. But, the real heartbreak of this sad day will be seeing our generation, our friends, our loved ones, who died without Christ.

We will know then what could have been. Then we will see the truth of what God said in His Word when He said, "I have set thee a watchman… therefore thou shalt hear the word at my mouth, and warn them from me. When I say unto the wicked, O wicked *man*, thou shalt surely die; if <u>thou dost not speak to warn</u> the wicked from his way, that wicked *man* shall die in his iniquity; but <u>his blood will I require at thine hand</u>.

Nevertheless, if thou warn the wicked of his way to turn from it; if he do not turn from his way, he shall die in his iniquity; but thou hast delivered thy soul." Ezekiel 33:7-8.

Every generation of Christians are responsible to give their generation the Gospel.

There will be tears and heart break beyond anything we have ever known, or experienced, because of our failure to give our generation the Gospel. When we see the lost, from the age's past, cast into the Lake of Fire, we will know what could have been. This will be the last time we ever see the unsaved. This is their final goodbye. They will be lost forever. We who know the Lord as our personal Saviour, will witness this tragic day.

THE GREAT WHITE THRONE JUDGEMENT

The Lord Jesus is the One who sits on the throne. He said, "For the Father judgeth no man, but hath committed all judgment unto the Son: That all men should honour the Son, even as they honour the Father. He that honoureth not the Son honoureth not the Father which hath sent Him." John 5:22-23.

This judgement is after the thousand-year reign of Christ. The Bible says, "But the rest of the dead lived not again until the thousand years were finished.

This is the first resurrection." Revelation 20:5. After being with Christ, for a 1000 years, we will only begin to understand the great loss of those who die without Christ

The Bible says, "And I saw a great white throne, and Him that sat on it, from whose face the earth and the heaven fled away; and there was found no place for them." Revelation 20:11.

This judgment will take place somewhere other than heaven or earth. Heaven and earth have seen a lot, but they will not be able to witness this.

"And I saw the dead, small and great, stand before God...And the sea gave up the dead which were in it; and death and hell delivered up the dead which were in them: and they were judged every man according to their works... "And the sea gave up the dead which were in it; and death and hell delivered up the dead which were in them: and they were judged every man according to their works." Revelation 20:11,13-15.

★ ★ ★ ★ ★

Every person who has ever lived and died, in a lost condition, stands before God at this judgement.

The Lord Jesus said about this day, "Many will say to me in that day, Lord, Lord, have we not prophesied in thy name? and in thy name have cast out devils? and in thy name done many wonderful works?

And then will I profess unto them, I never knew you: depart from Me, ye that work iniquity." Matthew 7:22-23.

Death And Hell Cast Into The Lake Of Fife

The Bible says, "And death and hell were cast into the lake of fire. This is the second death. And whosoever was not found written in the book of life was cast into the lake of fire." Revelation 20:12-15.

Their sin is not under the blood. All their thoughts and deeds are revealed. They will also see that their name is not written in the Lamb's book of life.

The Result of This Judgment?

"...And whosoever was not found written in the book of life was cast into the lake of fire." Revelation 20:13-15. "Then shall He say also unto them on the left hand, Depart from Me, ye cursed, into everlasting fire, prepared for the devil and his angels." Matthew 25:41.

THE GREAT WHITE THRONE JUDGEMENT

The saddest day in human history is when Jesus says, "Depart from Me…" and they are cast into the lake of fire. Without God's grace we would not be able to bear the pain and suffering that we will witness on that day. When we see our friends and loved ones cast into the lake of fire, we will wish we had done more to reach them.

The Bible says, "And whosoever was not found written in the book of life was cast into the lake of fire." Revelation 20:15. No wonder Jesus told His disciples to, "rejoice because your names are written in heaven." Luke 10:20.

> "Rejoice because your
> Names are written in Heaven."
>
> Luke 10:20

★ ★ ★ ★ ★

Seeing the **FUTURE**

Hell, A Prepared Place For The Devil

Jesus said, "Wherefore if thy hand or thy foot offend thee, cut them off, and cast them from thee: it is better for thee to enter into life halt or maimed, rather than having two hands or two feet to be cast into everlasting fire. And if thine eye offend thee, pluck it out, and cast it from thee: it is better for thee to enter into life with one eye, rather than having two eyes to be cast into hell fire." Matthew 18:8-9.

You do not hear much about Hell today, unless you hear someone who is making a joke about it. Sad to say, many Christians have put it out of their minds. Quite often, the subject of Hell and eternal torment is never mentioned from our pulpits. Did Hell disappear? Did it go away? What happened to Hell? If the Lord Jesus were walking this earth today, would He discuss it as often as He did when He came?

Seeing the FUTURE

There is one thing for sure, and that is that Hell and eternal punishment is not a popular message in our day. The truth about Hell, and the Lake of Fire, are forgotten messages of the Bible. We may ignore the subject of Hell altogether, but it does not go away. The Bible says, "Hell hath enlarged herself, and opened her mouth without measure..." Isaiah 5:14.

You ask, "How is that possible? How can Hell be growing?" Jesus said more people are going to Hell than are going to Heaven. He said, "Enter ye in at the strait gate: for wide *is* the gate, and broad *is* the way, that leadeth to destruction, and many there be which go in there at:" Matthew 7:13.

Hell is growing every day and at a faster pace than ever before in human history. Think with me as we consider some important questions on this subject.

Hell Is A Real Place. David talked about Hell. He said, "If I ascend up into heaven, Thou art there: if I make my bed in hell, behold, Thou art there." Psalm 139:8. Hell is a real place just like Heaven is a real place. Jesus said, "And thou, Capernaum, which art exalted to heaven, shalt be thrust down to hell." Luke 10:15.

The Lord Jesus spoke of Heaven being above and Hell being beneath. Heaven is above. Jesus said, "He that cometh from above is above all...He that cometh from heaven is above all." John 3:31. Hell is beneath. The Bible says, "Hell from beneath is moved for thee to meet..." Isaiah 14:9.

Hell was "prepared for the devil and his angels:" Matthew 25:41. Hell will one day be cast into the lake of fire. The Bible says, "And death and hell were cast into the lake of fire. This is the second death." Revelation 20:14. I try to always remind people that Hell was prepared for the devil and his angels, that is why I often refer to Hell as, "The Devils Hell."

When Satan fell, he took one-third of the angels in Heaven with him. The Bible says about the fall of Satan, "And his tail drew the third part of the stars of heaven, and did cast them to the earth... And the great dragon was cast out, that old serpent, called the Devil, and Satan, which deceiveth the whole world: he was cast out into the earth, and his angels were cast out with him." Revelation 12:4,9.

Some of these fallen angels are being held in Hell until their day of judgment. Peter said, "For if God spared not the angels that sinned, but cast them down to hell, and delivered them into chains of darkness, to be reserved unto judgment." II Peter 2:4. We can only imagine how wicked these angels, who are chained in darkness, are.

God prepared Heaven for people, not Hell. Jesus said, "In My Father's house are many mansions: if it were not so, I would have told you. I go to prepare a place for you." John 14:2. God does not want people to go to the place He has prepared for the devil and his angels. One day, Satan and all who rebelled with him will be cast into Hell. Who would want to be in the same place with Satan?

★ ★ ★ ★ ★

Hell Is A Place Of Torment. Jesus told us about a man who died and went to Hell. He told us what this man said Hell was like. The man "cried and said, Father Abraham, have mercy on me, and send Lazarus, that he may dip the tip of his finger in water, and cool my tongue; for I am tormented in this flame." Luke 16:24.

This man said Hell is a place of torment, and he did not want his five brothers to end up in Hell. He asked if someone could go warn them, "lest they also come into this place of torment." Luke 16:18. People who die and go to Hell do not want others to follow them there.

The Bible teaches us that the Devil and his angles "shall be tormented day and night for ever and ever." Revelation 20:10.

Hell is a place of unquenchable, and everlasting fire. Jesus said Hell is a "fire that never shall be quenched:" Mark 9:43. He also said Hell is a, "everlasting fire" Matthew 25:41. The rich man who died and went to a devil's Hell said, "…I am tormented in this flame" Luke 16:24. Hell is a place of separation and loneliness. The rich man knew that he would be separated from his family and loved ones forever. He also knew that if they came to that awful place, they would not be together, because Hell is a place of loneliness.

It is a place of sorrow. The Bible says "The sorrows of hell compassed me about: the snares of death prevented me." Psalm 18:5. The rich man who died and went to Hell could feel, remember, desire, and speak, but nothing could be done.

Who Is Going To Hell?

Jesus said more people are dying and going to a devil's Hell than are going to Heaven. He said, "… for wide is the gate, and broad is the way, that leadeth to destruction, and many there be which go in there at:" Matthew 7:13.

Think about this. According to Jesus, more people that we meet are going to a devil's Hell than are going to Heaven. No wonder the Bible says, "Therefore hell hath enlarged herself…" Isaiah 5:14.

We must always remember, "The Lord is not slack concerning his promise, as some men count slackness; but is longsuffering to us-ward, not willing that any should perish, but that all should come to repentance." II Peter 3:9. In other words, God does not want anyone to die and go to a devil's Hell. He wants everyone to go to Heaven when they die. It is for that reason Jesus died on Calvary.

★ ★ ★ ★ ★

Seeing the FUTURE

Beyond Death

"And as it is appointed unto men once to die, but after this the judgment:" Hebrews 9:27.

Is it possible to see into your future? Is it possible to know what is coming next for you?

The answer may shock you, but YES; it is possible to see into your future. God's Word tells us what is next beyond death. We all have an appointment with death, "It is appointed unto men once to die." The Bible says, "but after this." What will be your, "after this" life's future?

When God made Adam, He created him to live forever. Man is a living soul. The Bible says, "And the LORD God formed man of the dust of the ground and breathed into his nostrils the breath of life; and man became "<u>a living soul</u>." Gensis 2:7.

Man is not like any other creation, because man is body, soul, and spirit. Paul, when writing the Thessalonians said, "And the very God of peace sanctify you wholly; and I pray God your whole <u>spirit</u> and <u>soul</u> and <u>body</u> be preserved blameless unto the coming of our Lord Jesus Christ." Thessalonians 5:23.

Humans are eternal beings. When someone dies, only their body dies because we are eternal, living souls. That means everyone who has lived is still alive, somewhere, according to the Bible.

★★★★★

Seeing the FUTURE

When Christians die the Bible says, "We are confident, I say, and willing rather to be absent from the body, and to be present with the Lord." II Corinthians 5:8.

Jesus said, "I go and prepare a place for you... that where I am, there ye may be also." Heaven is a place with beauty beyond our wildest dreams.

Jesus is the only door to Heaven. Jesus said, "I am the door: by me if any man enter in, he shall be saved." Jesus died for our sins and paid our sin debt in full. Jesus rose from the grave. He said, "Because I live ye shall live also."

Jesus said, "I am the resurrection, and the life: he that believeth in me, though he were dead, yet shall he live: And whosoever liveth and believeth in me shall <u>never die</u>."

Jesus said believers "never die." Their body dies, but believers have everlasting life. They do not die. They close their eyes in death and open them in Heaven. In death Christians are "absent from the body, and...present with the Lord."

Everyone is going to live forever somewhere; one day we will see it is true. Is Heaven going to be your eternal home when you die?

When unbelievers die the Bible says, "The rich man also died, and was buried; And in hell he lift up his eyes, being in torments..." Luke 16:22-23. Why was Hell prepared? "Then shall He say also unto them on the left hand, Depart from Me, ye cursed, into everlasting fire, prepared for the devil and his angels:" Matthew 25:41.

BEYOND DEATH

Everyone who has ever lived is in one of two places. If they were believers, they are in Heaven with Jesus. If they were <u>not</u> believers, they are in a place God prepared for the devil and his angels, they are in a devils Hell. According to the Bible there are no dead people, or their spirits, walking around. Would you like to know what is beyond death for you?

In 100 years, everyone who is alive today will be in their "after this" future. Do you want your after this to be spent in Heaven? I have good news. Jesus is the only Eternity Planner, and when He was here, He told us how to go to Heaven when our appointment with death comes.

Jesus said, "In my Father's house are many mansions...I go to prepare a place for you...that where I am, there ye may be also...I am the way, the truth, and the life: no man cometh unto the Father, but by me." John 14:1-6.

> "We are confident...and willing...
>
> To be absent from the body,
>
> And to be present with the Lord."
>
> II Corinthians 5:8

> "Rejoice, because your names are written in Heaven."
>
> Luke 10:20

★ ★ ★ ★ ★

Seeing the **FUTURE**

Death Has Been Defeated

Everything about death changed when Jesus rose from the grave. In the Old Testament the Psalmist said, "Yea, though I walk through the valley of the shadow of death, I will fear no evil: for thou art with me; thy rod and thy staff they comfort me." Psalm 23:4.

There are no valleys and no shadows in death, for the believer, since Jesus rose from the grave. **Death has been defeated**. Jesus said, "I am he that liveth, and was dead; and, behold, I am alive for evermore, Amen; and have the keys of hell and of death." Revelation 1:18.

There is no fear in death for the child of God.

The Bible says that in death we are "absent from the body, and…present with the Lord." II Corinthians 5:8. Jesus said Christians never die. He said to Martha, "I am the resurrection, and the life: he that believeth in me, though he were dead, yet shall he live: And whosoever liveth and believeth in me shall never die. Believest thou this?" John 11:25-26.

★ ★ ★ ★ ★

God created man in His image. God made man a living soul. (Genesis 2:7) Man is "spirit and soul and body."
I Thessalonians 5:23.

When our body dies, we do not die. Everyone who has ever lived is still alive today somewhere in their forever. For the child of God their forever home is Heaven.

In the book of Job this question is asked. "If a man die shall he live again?" Job 14:14. God did not answer the question in the Old Testament, but Jesus did.

He told Martha "whosoever liveth and believeth in me shall never die." John 11:26. A Christian never dies.

Jesus said we will not even see death.

Jesus said to His followers, "Verily, verily, I say unto you, If a man keep my saying, he shall never see death." John 8:51. Our body dies, but we never die, and we do not see death when we die.

We see our friends and love ones who die, in the faith, close their eyes and leave this world in death. But what we see, they do not see.

DEATH HAS BEEN DEFEATED

We see what happens on the outside because man looks on the outside. But the one dying does not see what we see, they see Jesus. In other words, they leave their body behind in death because God will one day give them a glorious new body.

When Steven was put to death for preaching the Gospel, he said "Behold, I see the heavens opened, and the Son of man standing on the right hand of God." Acts 7:56.

Steven did not see his body dying he saw Jesus standing to welcome him home. When our loved ones leave this world, in death, they do not see what others around them see. They see Jesus standing to welcome them home to Heaven. Heaven is God's gift to His children.

> "Jesus…delivered us from
>
> The wrath to come."
>
> I Thessalonians 1:10

Seeing the **FUTURE**

Heaven, Is God's Gift To Believers

Jesus said, "I go and prepare a place for you... that where I am, there ye may be also." John 14:3. Heaven is a place with beauty beyond our wildest dreams.

Jesus is the only door to Heaven. Jesus said, "I am the door: by me if any man enter in, he shall be saved." John 10:9. Jesus died for our sins and paid our sin debt in full. Jesus rose from the grave. He said, "Because I live ye shall live also." John 10:7. "Jesus said...I am the resurrection, and the life: he that believeth in me, though he were dead, yet shall he live: And whosoever liveth and believeth in me shall <u>never die</u>." John 11:25-26.

Jesus said believers "never die." Their body dies, but believers have everlasting life. They do not die. They close their eyes in death and open them in Heaven. In death Christians are "absent from the body, and...present with the Lord." II Corinthians 5:8. Everyone is going to live forever somewhere; one day we will see it is true. Is Heaven going to be your eternal home when you die?

★★★★★

You Can Go To Heaven

Acknowledge you are a sinner. The Bible says, "As it is written, There is none righteous, no, not one…For all have sinned, and come short of the glory of God;" Romans 3:10,23.

Believe Christ died for you. The Bible says, "For the wages of sin is death; but the gift of God is eternal life through Jesus Christ our Lord." Romans 6:23 "God commendeth His love toward us, in that, while we were yet sinners, Christ died for us." Romans 5:8

Call upon Him to save you. The Bible says, "That if thou shalt confess with thy mouth the Lord Jesus, and shalt believe in thine heart that God hath raised him from the dead, thou shalt be saved." Romans 10:9.

If you would be willing to turn to God in repentance and faith, pray this prayer: "Lord, I know that I am a sinner, and I believe You died and rose again for me. I am trusting you to forgive me. Come into my heart and save me, and help me to live for you. In Jesus' name I pray, Amen."

Everlasting life is ours when we receive Christ as our personal Saviour. God bless you.

"Let not your heart be troubled:

Ye believe in God, believe also in me.

In my Father's house are many mansions:

If *it were* not *so*, I would have told you.

I go to prepare a place for you.

And if I go and prepare a place for you,

I will come again, and receive you unto myself;

That where I am, *there* ye may be also."

John 14:1-3

★ ★ ★ ★ ★

Seeing the FUTURE

Heaven
By Tom Sexton

There are no shadows in death with Jesus.

There are no valleys we must walk through.

Death is only a doorway,

And all of **Heaven** awaits you.

Our vision on earth is limited -

We see only into the blue,

But in death our vision is endless -

All of Glory comes into view.

Death takes hold of the body,

And our race on earth is through.

The battle for us is over.

With open arms He welcomes you.

So, fear not the end of life's journey.

Believe what God says is true.

Death has been defeated!

Heaven is His gift to you.

Are We Living In The Last Days?

> "This know also, that in the last days perilous times shall come." II Timothy 3:1.

The Bible says, "Knowing this first, that there shall come in the last days scoffers, walking after their own lusts, And...in the latter times some shall depart from the faith, giving heed to seducing spirits, and doctrines of devils; Speaking lies in hypocrisy...." II Peter 3:3-4, I Timothy 4:1-3,

The question that every serious-minded Christian should determine to find the answer to is this, "Are we living in the last days?" As we look in God's Word, for the answer to this question, let us remember that there are no signs for the Rapture of the church, but there are signs for the Second Coming of Christ. Understanding these two different events helps us to know that we are truly living in the last days.

What are some signs that show we are living in the last days of the Church age.

★ ★ ★ ★ ★

Increase In Wars And Rumors Of War

"And when ye shall hear of wars and rumours of wars, be ye not troubled: for such things must needs be; but the end shall not be yet." Mark 13:7.

As we approach the end of the Church age there shall be wars and rumors of more wars. Never in the history of human events has there been more wars and the talk of preparing for war.

Extreme Materialism

"This know also, that in the last days perilous times shall come. For men shall be lovers of their own selves, covetous, boasters, proud, blasphemers, disobedient to parents, unthankful, unholy." II Timothy 3:1-2.

As we approach the end of the Church age there will be a desire to have more and more of what the world offers for oneself. "For men shall be lovers of their own selves…" We are warned not to love the world or anything that is of the world. (I John 2:15-17)

Lawlessness

"Perilous times shall come." These perilous times describe a people who do not care about others or the laws that govern people. We are fast approaching a time in our nation where men do what is right in their own eyes and justify their misbehavior and crimes against others.

An Increase In Speed And Knowledge

"But thou, O Daniel, shut up the words, and seal the book, even to the time of the end: many shall <u>run to and fro</u>, and <u>knowledge shall be increased</u>." Daniel 12:4.

Daniel describes the end as a time people travel by speed, and a time when knowledge shall increase. Today it is possible to travel around the world quickly and with considerable ease compared to Bible times. The computer has brought the four corners of the earth closer. A vast amount of knowledge is available to anyone who has a computer.

Unification Of The World's Systems

"The kings of the earth set themselves, and the rulers take counsel together, against the LORD, and against his anointed..." Psalm 2:2.

"And all that dwell upon the earth shall worship him, whose names are not written in the book of life of the Lamb slain from the foundation of the world." Revelation 13:8.

These verses are talking about the world system after the Rapture of the church, a time when all world government will come together as one.

★ ★ ★ ★ ★

We hear today of the expression "one world order." There are many who believe that the only way to have peace is to have one world order (Illustration: United Nations). This is the revival of the old Roman Empire spoken of by Daniel. (Daniel 2:41, 7:7-8, Revelation 13:1, 17:12)

A Departure From The Christian Faith

"Now the Spirit speaketh expressly, that in the latter times some shall depart from the faith.." I Timothy 4:1.

"Let no man deceive you by any means: for that day shall not come, except there come a falling away first, and that man of sin be revealed, the son of perdition." II Thessalonians 2:3, (II Timothy 4:3-4, II Peter 3:3-4; I John 2:19) The Bible says that there shall be a "falling away."

This means that the end times can be identified by a departure from the Christian faith. Our nation, that was once a Christian nation, is now sadly a nation of many gods.

Increase In Demonic Activity

"Now the Spirit speaketh expressly, that in the latter times some shall depart from the faith, giving heed to seducing spirits, and doctrines of devils." I Timothy 4:1-3.

The closer we get to the coming of the Lord, the more active the spirit world becomes.

Never have so many of our young people had such an interest in the spiritual world. Many openly profess to be followers of Satan and his kingdom "...giving heed to seducing spirits, and doctrines of devils..."

Parents Without Natural Affection

"This know also, that in the last days perilous times shall come. For men shall be...Without natural affection, trucebreakers, false accusers, incontinent (without self-control), fierce, despisers of those that are good." II Timothy 3:3.

Many believe that this statement best describes the abortion movement. Millions of young women have believed the devil's lie that the child they were carrying was nothing more than a lifeless piece of flesh. Today we also hear of parents that take their children's life because they simply get tired of being tied down with them.

Abnormal Sexual Activities

"And as it was in the days of Noe, so shall it be also in the days of the Son of man. Likewise, also as it was in the days of Lot; they did eat, they drank, they bought, they sold, they planted, they builded." Luke 17:26, 28,

The Lord Jesus tells us that the days of Noah and the days of Lot will describe what the world will be like before His coming.

★ ★ ★ ★ ★

The days of Noah

"And God saw that the wickedness of man was great in the earth, and that every imagination of the thoughts of his heart was only evil continually." Genesis 6:5. There was a breakdown in the home (family) and open and abnormal sexual activity. Men and women's minds were totally given to this lifestyle.

The days of Lot

"And the LORD said, Because the cry of Sodom and Gomorrah is great, and because their sin is very grievous." Genesis 18:20. When the Lord Jesus reminded us about the days of Lot, He was not just telling us how the world would change, He was also telling us that believers would begin thinking like Lot. We live in a Gomorrah-minded world with many Lot-minded believers.

Hatred And Ridicule Of The Bible

"But, beloved, remember ye the words which were spoken before of the apostles of our Lord Jesus Christ; How that they told you there should be mockers in the last time, who should walk after their own ungodly lusts." Jude 1:17-18.

The Bible has always had its critics, but the end times are identified by an increase in "mockers" and "scoffers." II Peter 3:3. The Bible is the most criticized book of all time and has stood the test of time and the assault of scoffers.

The Restoration Of The Nation Of Israel

"And he shall set up an ensign for the nations, and shall assemble the outcasts of Israel, and gather together the dispersed of Judah from the four corners of the earth." Isaiah 11:12.

The developments in Israel and the Middle East are the most important signs that we are living in the last days. Israel is God's clock. As we watch these events unfold, that were prophesied in God's Word, we can know that we are truly living in the last days. There are many other signs that reveal to us that we are living in the last days. These are just a few. What should we do?" Pray for the peace of Jerusalem." Psalm 122:6.

"Jesus unto them...I am the door:

By me if any man enter in, he shall be

Saved...." John 10:7,9

Jesus said, "I am the way, the truth, and the life: No man cometh unto the Father,

but by Me." John 14:6

★ ★ ★ ★ ★

Seeing the FUTURE

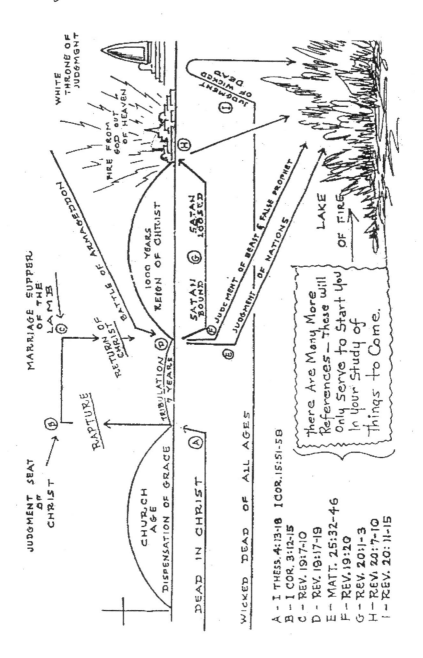

124

God Will Make All Things New And He Wants You There

God's desire has always been to spend eternity with us. This is when it begins. He wipes away the tears from our eyes (Revelation 21:4), and He makes all things new (Revelation 21:5). Do you know Jesus the only eternity planner?

Jesus

The Only Eternity Planner

Jesus said, "Lay not up for yourselves treasures upon earth, where moth and rust doth corrupt, and where thieves break through and steal: But lay up for yourselves treasures in heaven, where neither moth nor rust doth corrupt, and where thieves do not break through nor steal:" Matthew 6:19-20.

There are many who can help you plan for retirement, but there is only ONE who has planned your forever, and that my friend, is JESUS. Jesus truly is the world's only eternity planner.

So, with this in mind, what do you want in your next life? This life is "a vapour that appeareth for a little time, and then vanisheth away." James 4:14. Our next life is forever.

★ ★ ★ ★ ★

Seeing the **FUTURE**

Good news, Jesus is our future life planner. If people would listen to His advice, they would have a better forever. What advice does Jesus give concerning the forever life?

Make sure your name is on the official residence list of Heaven

Jesus said, "rejoice, because your names are written in heaven." Luke 10:20. Make sure your name is written in Heaven. The Bible says, "And whosoever was not found written in the book of life was cast into the lake of fire." Revelation 20:15. Our names are written in Heaven "in the Lamb's book of life" when we are born again.

If your name is written in Heaven, you will have a place to live. Jesus said, "In my Father's house are many mansions: if it were not so, I would have told you. I go to prepare a place for you." John 14:2.

Your heavenly home comes fully furnished and it has a great view. You are going to love living there.

Tell your family and friends how they can join you in Heaven

We read where "One of the two which heard John speak, and followed him, was Andrew, Simon Peter's brother.

The Bible says, "He first findeth his own brother Simon, and saith unto him, We have found the Messias, which is, being interpreted, the Christ. And he brought him to Jesus." John 1:40-41.

★ ★ ★ ★ ★

Six powerful words, "And he brought him to Jesus." Jesus encouraged Andrew to bring his brother to Him. Jesus wants families to be together in Heaven. If we will bring our family and friends to Jesus, He will take care of the rest.

Don't go to Heaven without telling the people you love how to know Christ as their personal Saviour.

Where do we begin? Begin by telling your family what the Lord has done for you and tell your friends the same.

Send some treasures ahead of you to Heaven.

Jesus said, "Lay not up for yourselves treasures upon earth, where moth and rust doth corrupt, and where thieves break through and steal: But lay up for yourselves treasures in heaven, where neither moth nor rust doth corrupt, and where thieves do not break through nor steal:" Matthew 6:19-20

Jesus said in Revelation 3:18, "buy of me gold." How much of Heavens "gold" is in your heavenly portfolio?

The only "treasures" we can take with us to Heaven are people. Do you know people who need to hear the Gospel? Invest in Heaven by investing in God's work. Your "treasures in heaven" will testify to your love for Jesus.

Be ready for your departure to Heaven

Jesus said, "Be therefore also ready: for in such an hour as ye think not the Son of man cometh."

Seeing the **FUTURE**

Matthew 24:44. When He comes, our time is up. There will be no time to say good-bye.

Our Heavenly treasure is "kept by the power of God." He protects it from "moth, rust" and "thieves." These are three things that have the power to destroy earthly treasures.

Our Heavenly treasure increases in value because people add to its worth by investing their lives in the Lord's work.

Paul encouraged the people, he reached with the Gospel, by saying, "Holding forth the word of life: that I may rejoice in the day of Christ, that I have not run in vain, neither laboured in vain." Philippians 2:16.

In other words, keep investing what you have been given, keep investing the Gospel. It was investing their lives in the Lord's work that made it gain in worth.

We grow to love our treasure in Heaven more as time goes on. We can truly say about the people that have influenced our lives, "I thank my God upon every remembrance of you," Philippians 1:3. What makes Heavens treasure so valuable is people we love are there. Do you have anyone or anything in Heaven you love?

Very few people think about "treasures in heaven." However, people do think about their retirement, which may never happen. Talk to your future planner, Jesus today, and ask Him about some investments you can make with your life.

★ ★ ★ ★ ★

You Can Go To Heaven

Acknowledge you are a sinner. The Bible says, "As it is written, There is none righteous, no, not one...For all have sinned, and come short of the glory of God;" Romans 3:10,23.

Believe Christ died for you. The Bible says, "For the wages of sin is death; but the gift of God is eternal life through Jesus Christ our Lord." "God commendeth His love toward us, in that, while we were yet sinners, Christ died for us." Romans 6:23, 5:8.

Call upon Him to save you. The Bible says, "That if thou shalt confess with thy mouth the Lord Jesus, and shalt believe in thine heart that God hath raised him from the dead, thou shalt be saved." Romans 10:9.

If you would be willing to turn to God in repentance and faith, pray this prayer: "Lord, I know that I am a sinner, and I believe You died and rose again for me. I am trusting you to forgive me. Come into my heart and save me, and help me to live for you. In Jesus' name I pray, Amen."

Everlasting life is ours when we receive Christ as our personal Saviour. God bless you.

★ ★ ★ ★ ★

For more helpful information and free downloads visit
www.FiveStarChristianMinistries.com